Scott Foresman Reading

Grade 3

Skills Tests
Teacher's Manual

Scott Foresman

Editorial Offices: Glenview, Illinois • New York, New York
Sales Offices: Reading, Massachusetts • Duluth, Georgia • Glenview, Illinois
Carrollton, Texas • Menlo Park, California

Editorial Offices
Glenview, Illinois • New York, New York

Sales Offices
Reading, Massachusetts • Duluth, Georgia • Glenview, Illinois
Carrollton, Texas • Menlo Park, California

ISBN 0-673-62454-4

5 6 7 8 9 10-BW-06 05 04 03 02

CONTENTS

OVERVIEW

Scott Foresman Reading provides a wide array of formal tests and classroom assessments to support instruction. Formal assessments include the following:

- Placement Tests
- Selection Tests
- Unit Skills Tests and End-of-Year Test
- Unit Benchmark Tests and End-of-Year Test

This Teacher's Manual provides information for administering the Skills Tests, scoring the tests, and interpreting the results. Detailed information about other assessment materials and procedures may be found in the *Assessment Handbook*.

Description of the Skills Tests

In Grade 3, there are six Unit Skills Tests—one for each unit—and an End-of-Year Test. The Unit Skills Tests are designed to measure a student's progress based on specific skills taught in each unit and to help you identify a student's specific strengths and weaknesses. Each Unit Skills Test has two parts: Reading and Writing/Study Skills. Each of these parts has two or three subtests.

The **Reading** part includes the following subtests:

- a Comprehension subtest that measures comprehension skills, vocabulary strategies, and literary genres and skills in relation to literature selections, including fiction, poetry, drama, nonfiction, and "functional" texts (posters, want ads, invitations, and the like)

- a Phonics subtest that measures phonics skills taught in the unit

The **Writing/Study Skills** part includes the following subtests:

- a Writing/Grammar subtest that measures grammar, usage, and mechanics skills taught in the unit, generally in the context of a written text

- a Writing prompt based on the targeted type of writing taught in the writing process activity in the unit

- a Study Skills subtest that measures study skills taught in the unit

The Unit Skills Tests are designed so that you may determine a separate score for each skill in the Reading subtests (Comprehension and Phonics); a separate score for each subtest; and a total test score. In Reading: Comprehension and Reading: Phonics, each skill is tested by at least four items. The Writing/Grammar and Study Skills subtests have a total of five to ten items each. All Skills Test questions are multiple-choice items, except for the Writing prompt.

The End-of-Year Skills Test follows the same design as the Unit Skills Test, but it is a longer test, and it measures selected skills from all six units taught during the year. It is designed to provide a score for each subtest and a total test score.

The design of the Skills Tests is the result of a two-year development effort, which included the administration of selected tests in a field tryout in the spring of 1998. Results from that field tryout, which involved a representative sample of students across the United States, were used to help refine the tests and ensure an appropriate level of difficulty.

USING THESE TESTS

The Skills Tests are designed for group administration in two or more sittings. Each Unit Skills Test in Grade 3 includes 55–60 test items organized in five subtests. These tests are not intended to be timed. We recommend allowing ample time for all students to complete the tests at their own rates. However, for the purposes of scheduling and planning, the chart below shows the number of items in each test and the estimated amount of time required to complete each section.

Unit Skills Test: Units 1–6		
Subtest	Number of Items	Estimated Time
Reading: Comprehension	20–24	30–35 minutes
Reading: Phonics	20–21	20 minutes
Writing/Grammar	5	5 minutes
Writing	1 Writing prompt	20 minutes
Study Skills	10	10 minutes

End-of-Year Skills Test		
Subtest	Number of Items	Estimated Time
Reading: Comprehension	25	40 minutes
Reading: Phonics	20	20 minutes
Writing/Grammar	10	10 minutes
Writing	1 Writing prompt	20–30 minutes
Study Skills	10	10 minutes

Each Unit Skills Test has four reading selections. The End-of-Year Skills Test has five reading selections.

ADMINISTERING THE TESTS

For each test in Grade 3, all questions except the Writing prompt are multiple-choice items with four answer choices. Each answer choice is indicated by a bubble.

Before you administer a test . . .

Review the test to familiarize yourself with the directions and the types of questions. Distribute a test to each student and make sure students have pencils for marking and writing their responses. Have students write their names on the front of the test and respond directly on the test pages by marking the letter for each answer. For the writing prompt, students should write their responses on the lined pages provided.

When you are ready to administer a test . . .

Students should read all test directions and answer the questions independently.

For each test that you administer, decide how many sessions to schedule. This decision will depend mainly on class schedules and how much testing your students can manage successfully in one session. If you choose to administer a Unit Skills Test in two sessions, you may want to test Reading in one session and Writing in another, as shown below:

Plan 1: Three Sittings	Plan 2: Two Sittings
1. Reading: Comprehension (30 minutes)	1. Reading: Comprehension (30 minutes) Reading: Phonics (20 minutes)

2. Reading: Phonics (20 minutes)
    Writing/Grammar (5 minutes)
	2. Writing/Grammar (5 minutes)
	    Writing prompt (20 minutes)
	    Study Skills (10 minutes)

3. Writing prompt (20 minutes) Study Skills (10 minutes)	

The directions for administering tests are designed to have students stop at the end of each subtest. Students will see a STOP sign at the bottom of the last page in each section. (If you want students to complete more than one subtest in a sitting, tell them which pages to complete before they stop.)

To begin a test, read the general directions below:

> General Directions
> **This is a test about reading and writing. Each question in the Reading section has four answer choices. Choose the best answer to each question and fill in the bubble beside your answer. In the Writing section, you will answer some questions about language and you will respond to a writing prompt by writing a short composition.**

Tell students which part(s) of the test they will be expected to complete in each session and how much time they have. Then direct students to open their tests, read the directions, and answer the questions.

After testing . . .

Directions for scoring the tests follow. Answer Keys for all tests are in the back of this Teacher's Manual.

SCORING THE TESTS

All Skills Tests are intended to be scored by subtest and total test. In the Unit Tests, the Reading: Comprehension and Reading: Phonics subtests may also be scored by skill. (For a sample, see page T5.)

A total score for the Reading part of the test can be determined by adding together the scores for Reading: Comprehension and Reading: Phonics.

A score for the total test can be determined by adding together the numbers for all subtests except the Writing prompt, which is scored separately.

Scoring Multiple-Choice Items

Each multiple-choice item has four answer choices. Referring to the Answer Key for the test, mark each multiple-choice item correct or incorrect.

Scoring the Writing Activity

The Writing activity requires students to produce a written response. To evaluate the students' responses, read the writing prompt. Then, to score a response, review the Scoring Guide provided in the Answer Key. Read the student's writing and score it on a scale of 1 to 4, based on the criteria described in the Answer Key.

The criteria provided in each Scoring Guide are based on the key features of specific kinds of writing—as they have been taught in the writing process activities. The 4-point scale reflects the general levels of performance defined below; these levels are defined more specifically for each Writing activity.

Scoring Guides: 4-Point Scale

4   Exemplary

An "exemplary" response includes all the key features required for the specific type of writing. Errors in grammar, usage, and mechanics are minimal and do not prevent understanding.

3   Competent

A "competent" response includes most of the key features required for the specific type of writing. It may include a few errors in grammar, usage, and mechanics, but they do not prevent understanding.

2   Developing

A "developing" response includes some key features required for the specific type of writing. It may include several errors in grammar, usage, and mechanics, which may prevent understanding.

1   Emerging

An "emerging" response needs improvement. It does not include key features required for the specific type of writing. Errors in grammar, usage, and mechanics prevent understanding.

Using an Evaluation Chart

On pages T10–T16 are seven Evaluation Charts: one for each Unit Skills Test and one for the End-of-Year Skills Test. On page T17 is a Class Record Chart for recording test scores from all students.

To score a Skills Test using an Evaluation Chart, we recommend the following procedure:

1. Make a copy of the appropriate Evaluation Chart for each student.
2. Refer to the Answer Key for the test you are scoring.
3. For multiple-choice questions, mark the response to each question correct or incorrect. On the Evaluation Chart, circle the question number for each item answered correctly. Draw an X through the number of each question answered incorrectly.
4. To find the total score for a subtest, skill, or total test, add the number of items answered correctly. A total score for the test can be determined by adding together the numbers for all subtests except the Writing prompt, which is scored separately.
5. To determine a percentage score for the number of items answered correctly—by subtest, by skill, or by total test—use one of the tables on pages T6–T7.

The sample below shows scoring for each Reading: Comprehension skill included in one Unit Skills Test (Character, Cause and effect, and so on).

SUBTEST Skill/Item Numbers					Number Correct	%
READING: Comprehension						
Character	①	③	~~14~~	⑬	3/4	75%
Cause and effect	②	⑥	⑫	~~18~~	3/4	75%
Author's purpose	④	~~9~~	~~14~~	⑲	2/4	50%
Drawing conclusions	~~7~~	⑧	⑯	⑰	3/4	75%
Vocabulary: Unfamiliar words	⑤	⑩	⑮	⑳	4/4	75%
Total Comprehension					15/20	75%

6. For the Writing activity, review the Scoring Guide provided in the Answer Key. Then read the student's writing and score it on a scale of 1 to 4, based on the criteria described in the Key.
7. Mark the student's score for writing on the Evaluation Chart. Add any notes or observations about the writing that may be helpful to you and the student in later instruction.

Percentage Scores

Tables 1 and 2 that follow show percentage scores for Unit Skills Tests—by subtest and by skill, respectively. Table 3 shows percentage scores for the End-of-Year Test.

To find a percentage score by subtest in Table 1, locate the number of items answered correctly in the "Number Correct" column. Then go across to the column for the subtest you are scoring. For example, a student who answers 15 of 20 items correctly in Reading: Comprehension has achieved a percentage score of 75%. (Note that the number of items in Comprehension varies from 20 to 24 in different units, the number of items in Phonics varies from 20 to 21; thus, the total number of items in Reading may vary from 40 to 45.)

Table 1. Percentage Scores for Subtests in the Unit Skills Tests

Number Correct	Reading: Comprehension		Reading: Phonics		TOTAL READING		Writing/ Grammar	Study Skills
	20 items	24 items	20 items	21 items	40 items	45 items		
1	5%	4%	5%	5%	3%	2%	20%	10%
2	10%	8%	10%	10%	5%	4%	40%	20%
3	15%	13%	15%	14%	8%	7%	60%	30%
4	20%	17%	20%	19%	10%	9%	80%	40%
5	25%	21%	25%	24%	13%	11%	100%	50%
6	30%	25%	30%	29%	15%	13%		60%
7	35%	29%	35%	33%	18%	16%		70%
8	40%	33%	40%	38%	20%	18%		80%
9	45%	38%	45%	43%	23%	20%		90%
10	50%	42%	50%	48%	25%	22%		100%
11	55%	46%	55%	52%	28%	24%		
12	60%	50%	60%	57%	30%	27%		
13	65%	54%	65%	62%	33%	29%		
14	70%	58%	70%	67%	35%	31%		
15	75%	63%	75%	71%	38%	33%		
16	80%	67%	80%	76%	40%	36%		
17	85%	71%	85%	81%	43%	38%		
18	90%	75%	90%	86%	45%	40%		
19	95%	79%	95%	90%	48%	42%		
20	100%	83%	100%	95%	50%	44%		
21		88%		100%	53%	47%		
22		92%			55%	49%		
23		96%			58%	51%		
24		100%			60%	53%		
25					63%	56%		
26					65%	58%		
27					68%	60%		
28					70%	62%		
29					73%	64%		
30					75%	67%		
31					78%	69%		
32					80%	71%		
33					83%	73%		
34					85%	76%		
35					88%	78%		
36					90%	80%		
37					93%	82%		
38					95%	84%		
39					98%	87%		
40					100%	89%		
41						91%		
42						93%		
43						96%		
44						98%		
45						100%		

Table 2. Percentage Scores for Individual Skills in the Unit Skills Tests

Number Correct	Skill (4 items)	Skill (5 items)	Skill (8 items)
1	25%	20%	13%
2	50%	40%	25%
3	75%	60%	38%
4	100%	80%	50%
5		100%	63%
6			75%
7			88%
8			100%

To find a percentage score by skill in Table 2, locate the number of items answered correctly in the "Number Correct" column. Then go across to the column for the number of items per skill (which may be 4, 5, or 8, depending on the skill). For example, a student who answers 3 of 4 items correctly for a skill measured by 4 items has achieved a percentage score of 75%.

Table 3. Percentage Scores by Subtest for End-of-Year Skills Test

Number Correct	Reading: Comprehension	Reading: Phonics	Writing/Grammar or Study Skills
1	4%	5%	10%
2	8%	10%	20%
3	12%	15%	30%
4	16%	20%	40%
5	20%	25%	50%
6	24%	30%	60%
7	28%	35%	70%
8	32%	40%	80%
9	36%	45%	90%
10	40%	50%	100%
11	44%	55%	
12	48%	60%	
13	52%	65%	
14	56%	70%	
15	60%	75%	
16	64%	80%	
17	68%	85%	
18	72%	90%	
19	76%	95%	
20	80%	100%	
21	84%		
22	88%		
23	92%		
24	96%		
25	100%		

To find a percentage score by subtest in Table 3, locate the number of items answered correctly in the "Number Correct" column. Then go across to the column for the subtest you are scoring. For example, a student who answers 24 of 25 items correctly in Reading: Comprehension has achieved a percentage score of 96%.

To determine the percentage score for a total test, find the total number of items answered correctly. Divide the total number correct by the total number of items on the test. For example, the Unit 1 Skills Test has a total of 55 multiple-choice items. Suppose a student answers a total of 44 items correctly: $44 \div 55 = 0.80$, or 80%.

Interpreting Test Results

A student's score on the Skills Test provides only one look at a student's developmental progress and should be interpreted in conjunction with other assessments and the teacher's observations. However, a low score on one or more parts of the Skills Test probably indicates a need for closer review of the student's performance and perhaps additional instruction.

For these Skills Tests, we recommend a passing score of at least 70% on each subtest (Reading: Comprehension; Reading: Phonics; Writing/Grammar; and Study Skills) and, for a response to the Writing prompt, a score of at least 2 on the 4-point scale. If you score the Reading: Comprehension subtest by skill, students should achieve a score of at least 70% for each skill. (The Evaluation Chart for each Unit Skills Test lists the test items by skill.)

For a student who does not achieve these scores, you may want to review the student's test more carefully to identify which items the student answered incorrectly and to determine skills or specific areas in which the student needs additional help. The chart below is intended to provide guidelines for making instructional decisions based on Skills Test scores. Unless otherwise specified, all activities listed may be found in the Teacher's Guide.

Interpreting Test Scores

Students who score *90% or higher* on each subtest and on each skill . . .	**. . . need to be challenged.** An instructional plan might include: • Meeting Diverse Needs: Challenge activities to enhance the skills of students who perform at high levels • Leveled Readers Set C (challenge) to provide experience with target comprehension skills at a more challenging reading level
Students who score *70%–89%* on each subtest and on each skill . . .	**. . . need additional instructional support.** An instructional plan might include: • "If . . . then . . ." suggestions to guide instruction as indicated • Review skill lessons to maintain previously introduced phonics and comprehension skills • Daily Word Routines to provide quick phonics, vocabulary, and language arts practice • Leveled Readers Set B (easy/average) to reinforce comprehension skills and practice tested words • Phonics Readers to reinforce target phonics skills and to practice decoding in context

Students who score *below 70%* on any subtest *or* on any skill . . .	. . . need frequent teacher support and may need intervention.
	An instructional plan might include:
	• Ongoing Assessment: "If . . . then . . ." suggestions to guide instruction for students as they experience difficulty
	• Part 3 Comprehension lesson, which reteaches the target skill by breaking it into its component parts and applying it to less demanding text
	• Skills in Context to provide additional skill instruction and modeling
	• Meeting Diverse Needs: Intervention activities to provide intervention in oral language, comprehension, word study, and fluency
	• Leveled Readers Set A (easy) and Set B (easy/average) to reinforce comprehension skills and practice tested words

A student who scores low on one skill but reasonably well on the total subtest may need special attention in one or more areas. For example, a student might answer 15 of 20 Reading: Comprehension items correctly for a subtest score of 75%. However, within that subtest, the student may have answered incorrectly on all four test items measuring "Main idea," which may indicate a need for additional help in this area.

For any student whose Skills Test scores are not clearly definitive, we recommend administering additional assessments, such as the Individual Reading Inventory. For more information about other assessments, refer to the *Assessment Handbook*.

Grading. If you would like more information on how to a writing assessment scale for determining grades, refer to the "Grading Writing" section of the *Assessment Handbook*.

Evaluation Chart

Student Name _____ Date _____

SUBTEST Skill/Item Numbers					Number Correct	%
READING: Comprehension						
Character	1	3	11	13		
Cause and effect	2	6	12	18		
Author's purpose	4	9	14	19		
Drawing conclusions	7	8	16	17		
Vocabulary: Unfamiliar words	5	10	15	20		
Total Comprehension						
READING: Phonics						
Short vowels *a, e, i, o, u*	21	22	23	24		
	25	26	27	28		
Long vowels *a, e, i, o, u* and	29	30	31	32		
Vowel digraphs	33	34	35	36		
Double consonants	37	38	39	40		
Total Phonics						
TOTAL READING						
WRITING/GRAMMAR						
Sentences	1	2	3	4	5	
WRITING						
Personal Narrative		1	2	3	4	
STUDY SKILLS						
Parts of a book, Map	1	2	3	4	5
	6	7	8	9	10
TOTAL TEST (all multiple-choice items)						

Evaluation Chart

Student Name _____ Date _____

SUBTEST **Skill/Item Numbers**							Number Correct	%
READING: Comprehension								
Main idea and supporting details			6	10	11	13		
Graphic sources			7	8	14	15		
Realism and fantasy			2	4	16	18		
Context clues			1	5	9	19		
Vocabulary: Synonyms			3	12	17	20		
Total Comprehension								
READING: Phonics								
Consonants /j/g, j; /s/c, s		21	24	26	31	34		
Vowel digraphs oo, ou		22	25	28	30	33		
Diphthongs ou, ow		23	27	29	32	35		
Compound words		36	37	38	39	40		
Total Phonics								
TOTAL READING								
WRITING/GRAMMAR								
Nouns	1	2	3	4	5	6		
WRITING								
Descriptive			1	2	3	4		
STUDY SKILLS								
Dictionary, Alphabetical order		1	2	3	4	5		
		6	7	8	9	10		
TOTAL TEST (all multiple-choice items)								

Evaluation Chart

Student Name _____ Date _____

SUBTEST Skill/Item Numbers					Number Correct	%
READING: Comprehension						
Steps in a process	1	8	13	16		
Visualizing	3	7	14	19		
Sequence of events	4	6	11	18		
Summarizing	5	10	15	20		
Vocabulary: Multiple-meaning words	2	9	12	17		
Total Comprehension						
READING: Phonics						
r-controlled vowels	21	22	23	24		
Silent letters *wr, kn, st, gn, mb*	25	26	27	28		
Medial consonant digraphs *th, ch, ph, sh*	29	30	31	32		
Base words	33	34	35	36		
Suffixes *-ness, -ly, -ful, -ous*	37	38	39	40		
Total Phonics						
TOTAL READING						
WRITING/GRAMMAR						
Verbs	1	2	3	4	5	
WRITING						
Comparison/Contrast Paragraph		1	2	3	4	
STUDY SKILLS						
Encyclopedia, Evaluate reference	1	2	3	4	5	
source	6	7	8	9	10	
TOTAL TEST (all multiple-choice items)						

Student Name _____ Date _____

SUBTEST Skill/Item Numbers						Number Correct	%
READING: Comprehension							
Theme		1	5	7	12		
Setting		2	4	8	11		
Cause and effect		9	14	19	24		
Comparing and contrasting		15	16	21	23		
Literary device: idioms		6	17	18	22		
Vocabulary: Antonyms		3	10	13	20		
Total Comprehension							
READING: Phonics							
Diphthongs *oi, oy*		25	26	27	28		
r-controlled vowels		29	30	31	32		
Initial and final consonant blends		33	34	35	36		
Three-letter blends		37	38	39	40		
Possessives	41	42	43	44	45		
Total Phonics							
TOTAL READING							
WRITING/GRAMMAR							
Adjectives, Adverbs, Contractions, Capitalization	1	2	3	4	5		
WRITING							
How-To Report		1	2	3	4		
STUDY SKILLS							
Bar graphs, Circle graphs, Textbook	1	2	3	4	5		
	6	7	8	9	10		
TOTAL TEST (all multiple-choice items)							

Evaluation Chart

Student Name _____ Date _____

SUBTEST Skill/Item Numbers						Number Correct	%
READING: Comprehension							
Predicting		1	10	13	19		
Text structure		2	6	8	11		
Fact and opinion		3	5	7	9		
Author's purpose		4	12	16	22		
Literary devices: simile, metaphor		17	18	20	23		
Vocabulary: Homophones, homographs		14	15	21	24		
Total Comprehension							
READING: Phonics							
Consonant /k/c, ck, ch		25	28	29	32		
Digraph wh; /h/wh		26	27	30	31		
Prefixes im-, dis-, non-		33	34	35	36		
Inflected endings	37	38	39	40	41		
Plurals		42	43	44	45		
Total Phonics							
TOTAL READING							
WRITING/GRAMMAR							
Pronouns, Prepositions, Conjunctions	1	2	3	4	5		
WRITING							
Research Report		1	2	3	4		
STUDY SKILLS							
Atlas, Time line, Chart, Table	1	2	3	4	5		
	6	7	8	9	10		
TOTAL TEST (all multiple-choice items)							

Evaluation Chart

Student Name _____ Date _____

SUBTEST Skill/Item Numbers						Number Correct	%
READING: Comprehension							
Generalizing	1	3	14	17			
Making judgments	2	4	12	18			
Plot	6	9	13	19			
Setting	7	8	11	16			
Vocabulary: Multiple meaning words	5	10	15	20			
Total Comprehension							
READING: Phonics							
Vowel digraphs *ui, ew; au, aw;* /ò/*al*	21	22	23	24			
	25	26	27	28			
Affixes	29	30	31	32			
	33	34	35	36			
Syllabication	37	38	39	40			
Total Phonics							
TOTAL READING							
WRITING/GRAMMAR							
Compound sentences, punctuation, and subject-verb agreement	1	2	3	4	5		
WRITING							
Persuasive Letter		1	2	3	4		
STUDY SKILLS							
Poster/Announcement, Newspaper	1	2	3	4	5		
	6	7	8	9	10		
TOTAL TEST (all multiple-choice items)							

Evaluation Chart

Student Name _____ Date _____

SUBTEST Skill/Item Numbers					Number Correct	%
READING: Comprehension						
1	6	11	16	21		
2	7	12	17	22		
3	8	13	18	23		
4	9	14	19	24		
5	10	15	20	25		
READING: Phonics						
1	5	9	13	17		
2	6	10	14	18		
3	7	11	15	19		
4	8	12	16	20		
TOTAL READING						
WRITING/GRAMMAR						
1	3	5	7	9		
2	4	6	8	10		
WRITING Comparison/Contrast						
	1	2	3	4		
STUDY SKILLS						
1	3	5	7	9		
2	4	6	8	10		
TOTAL TEST (all multiple-choice items)						

CLASS RECORD

Teacher Name _____ Unit Skills Test _____

Directions: Use this chart to record results on a given Unit Skills Test for all students.

Student	Reading: Comprehension	Reading: Phonics	TOTAL READING	Writing/Grammar	Writing	Study Skills	TOTAL TEST

Unit 1 Skills Test

Finding My Place

Name _____

Date _____

Scott Foresman
Reading
Grade 3

Editorial Offices
Glenview, Illinois • New York, New York

Sales Offices
Reading, Massachusetts • Duluth, Georgia • Glenview, Illinois
Carrollton, Texas • Menlo Park, California

ISBN 0-673-62422-6

3 4 5 6 7 8 9 10-EBA-06 05 04 03 02 01

READING: Comprehension

DIRECTIONS

Read each passage. Then read each question about the passage. Choose the best answer to each question. Mark the space for your answer.

Asha's Blanket

Characters: Asha, an eight-year-old girl
Reth, her younger brother

Setting: Asha's bedroom

(Asha is lying on the bed reading. Reth walks into the room.)

RETH: I hate rainy days. There's nothing to do.

(Asha does not look up from her book. Reth wanders around the room looking at things. He opens the closet door, laughs, and takes an old blanket off a hook.)

RETH: Hey, Asha, you still can't sleep without your baby blankie?

ASHA: For your information, I haven't taken my blanket to bed for ages, but I still play with it. *(Reth looks puzzled. Asha takes the blanket from him, spreads it on the floor, and sits down on it.)* This is my magic carpet. Hop on and take a ride with me.

RETH: *(sitting down on blanket)* Where are we going?

ASHA: We're off to San Francisco.

RETH: *(looking over the edge of the blanket)* Look, there's the Golden Gate Bridge!

(Asha stands up and motions for Reth to do the same. She spreads the blanket over her desk and crawls under it. Reth crawls under too.)

RETH: What are we doing now?

ASHA: Shhh! We're explorers in the Old West. We've wandered into a grizzly bear's cave by mistake, and the bear is standing outside waiting for us!

RETH: *(nervously)* What should we do?

ASHA: Poof, he's gone! *(Asha laughs. Then she crawls out from under the desk and grabs the blanket. She* <u>drapes</u> *it over her shoulders and ties the ends around her neck.)*

RETH: Now what? Are you Superwoman, able to lift a car with one hand?

ASHA: *(standing tall and proudly)* Not quite. I am the Queen of Egypt, and you must obey my every command.

RETH: *(laughing)* Sorry, Queen. If I have to do whatever you command, then I think I've had enough of this game.

(Reth exits.)

1 How was Reth feeling when he walked into Asha's room?

- ○ bored
- ○ afraid
- ○ angry
- ○ excited

2 Asha spread the blanket on the floor because she wanted to —

- ○ lie on the blanket and read.
- ○ pretend it was a magic carpet.
- ○ live in San Francisco.
- ○ make Reth sit down.

3 What kind of person is Asha?

- ○ She is mean to her brother.
- ○ She thinks she knows everything.
- ○ She likes to play make-believe games.
- ○ She is serious all the time.

4 The author's purpose in this play is to —

- ○ give information about blankets.
- ○ describe a magic carpet.
- ○ compare a brother and sister.
- ○ tell a funny story about Asha and Reth.

5 In this play, the word <u>drapes</u> means —

- ○ hangs loosely; wraps.
- ○ folds into a small ball.
- ○ grabs quickly; takes.
- ○ ties in a knot.

GO ON

t Foresman 3

A Writer Grows Up

Cynthia Rylant grew up in a small town called Beaver in the mountains of West Virginia. When she was young, Cynthia had two wishes. She wanted to see the world beyond Beaver, and she wanted to do something important with her life.

As a child, Cynthia made friends and had adventures as she roamed around Beaver. She loved to see what was happening. She loved to hear what people said to one another. She watched, she listened, and she remembered.

As a young woman, Cynthia left Beaver and began writing stories for children. She had success almost right away, especially with her stories about Henry and his dog Mudge. Many of her stories were made into picture books, and she became famous. Since then, she has written dozens of books and won many awards.

Although Cynthia Rylant left Beaver, she never forgot it. The friends she made and the adventures she had there appear in almost all of her stories. When Cynthia was young, she could not know that Beaver would <u>provide</u> her everything she needed to do something important. But it did.

Some Books by Cynthia Rylant	
Title	**Date**
Night in the Country	1986
Henry and Mudge	1987
Missing May	1992
Poppleton	1997
Scarecrow	1998
The Troublesome Turtle	1999

GO ON

t Foresman 3

6 Cynthia Rylant wanted to leave Beaver to —
- ◯ forget her childhood.
- ◯ go to a new school.
- ◯ grow up.
- ◯ see other places.

7 Cynthia Rylant probably felt that she had done something important with her life when she —
- ◯ roamed around Beaver.
- ◯ won awards for her books.
- ◯ listened to her neighbors talk.
- ◯ made friends with other children.

8 What can you tell about Cynthia Rylant from this selection?
- ◯ She has been writing books since 1986.
- ◯ She loves her parents.
- ◯ She often goes to libraries.
- ◯ She lives in a big city far away from Beaver.

9 The author's purpose in this selection is to —
- ◯ describe West Virginia.
- ◯ teach children to write.
- ◯ give information about Cynthia Rylant.
- ◯ get people to visit Beaver.

10 In this selection, the word <u>provide</u> means —
- ◯ take.
- ◯ draw.
- ◯ give.
- ◯ learn.

GO ON

Annie Christmas

Back when our country was still young, there was a woman named Annie Christmas. Annie lived in the city of New Orleans beside the Mississippi River. People say that Annie was as strong as an ox. She was at least seven feet tall. When she yelled, the ground started shaking. But she did not yell very often. No one dared to bother her, so she didn't have much to yell about.

Annie Christmas had a boat on the Mississippi, and she worked harder than any ten men. She loaded things onto the boat and took them where they needed to go. Then she'd come back for another load. Night and day she worked, and she hardly ever stopped.

One day, a man named Mike Fink came to town. When he saw Annie Christmas, she was picking up a bale of hay to load onto the boat. Now Mike was a big strong man, but he was not very smart. He looked at Annie and laughed. "Why, Miss," he said, "you should be home making socks and not trying to do a man's work."

Well, the whole city went quiet, waiting to see what Annie would do.

Annie stood up slowly and looked at Mike Fink. "Mister," she said quietly, "you seem to have a lot to say about who should do what and where." Then she lifted that bale of hay over her head. Everyone thought she would throw it at Mike Fink, but she didn't. She threw it into the river so hard that it caused a tidal wave ten feet high. That tidal wave picked up Mike Fink and transported him all the way to Natchez, more than 150 miles away.

Annie went back to her work, and Mike Fink was never seen in New Orleans again.

t Foresman 3

11 What kind of person was Annie Christmas?
- ◯ peaceful
- ◯ hard-working
- ◯ shy
- ◯ nervous

12 Annie Christmas did not yell much because —
- ◯ her voice made the ground shake.
- ◯ she had work to do.
- ◯ no one dared to bother her.
- ◯ the city was quiet.

13 Which word best describes Mike Fink?
- ◯ foolish
- ◯ kind
- ◯ wise
- ◯ afraid

14 The author's purpose in this passage is to —
- ◯ entertain with a funny story.
- ◯ persuade people to visit New Orleans.
- ◯ describe the city of New Orleans.
- ◯ explain how to load a boat.

15 In this passage, the word transported means —
- ◯ yelled at.
- ◯ threw.
- ◯ hit hard.
- ◯ carried.

Party Time

On a cold day in October, Chet walked home from school. He was feeling lonesome. When he walked into the house, his mother called to him.

"Chet," she said, "you got a letter in the mail today."

"Me?" cried Chet as he raced toward the kitchen. "I got mail? Where is it?"

Mom was glad to see Chet so <u>thrilled</u>. She handed him the envelope. Chet ripped it open and began to read.

Dear Chet,

It is my favorite time of year again! Yes, it will soon be my birthday. You are invited to a birthday party.

Day: Friday, November 30
Time: 4:00 P.M. to 6:00 P.M.
Where: 24 Collins Road

There will be prizes for the funniest hats, lots of games to play, and great food to eat! I hope you can come.

Call 555-3457 to tell us you can be there.

Your friend,
Amy Barnes

GO ON

Foresman 3

16 What can you tell about Chet from this passage?
- ○ He has many friends.
- ○ He really likes Amy Barnes.
- ○ He does not like going to parties.
- ○ He does not get a lot of mail.

17 You can tell from the letter that kids who go to the party should —
- ○ bring food.
- ○ wear funny hats.
- ○ bring prizes.
- ○ eat before they get there.

18 Chet will win a prize if he —
- ○ plays a game.
- ○ calls 555-3457.
- ○ has one of the funniest hats.
- ○ eats the most food.

19 The purpose of Amy's letter is to —
- ○ invite friends to a party.
- ○ give directions to her house.
- ○ entertain with a silly story.
- ○ describe her hat.

20 In this passage, the word thrilled means —
- ○ out of breath.
- ○ excited.
- ○ sad and lonely.
- ○ cold.

STOP

t Foresman 3

READING: Phonics

DIRECTIONS
Read the word. Find the word that has the same sound as the underlined letter or letters. Mark the space for your answer.

21 dr<u>o</u>p

○ told   ○ rope   ○ lot   ○ pool

22 cl<u>a</u>ss

○ back   ○ bake   ○ beak   ○ bay

23 r<u>ou</u>gh

○ coat   ○ count   ○ cold   ○ cup

24 tr<u>i</u>p

○ pine   ○ pin   ○ pain   ○ pride

25 h<u>ea</u>d

○ seat   ○ rest   ○ star   ○ deep

26 b<u>u</u>s

○ mule   ○ mouse   ○ mount   ○ much

GO ON

t Foresman 3

27 t<u>e</u>nt
  ○ bread ○ bead ○ be ○ bean

28 m<u>u</u>st
  ○ true ○ tune ○ touch ○ turn

29 l<u>a</u>te
  ○ lamp ○ last ○ ball ○ rain

30 dr<u>ea</u>m
  ○ men ○ these ○ send ○ gray

31 n<u>i</u>ght
  ○ list ○ grin ○ ride ○ bird

32 m<u>u</u>sic
  ○ sun ○ burn ○ house ○ cute

33 th<u>ie</u>f
  ○ me ○ bed ○ her ○ met

34 cr<u>y</u>
  ○ stay ○ lie ○ you ○ crib

tt Foresman 3

35 st<u>o</u>ne

    ○ not   ○ stop   ○ more   ○ road

36 g<u>ai</u>n

    ○ ray   ○ fair   ○ land   ○ trap

37 s<u>u</u>per

    ○ phone   ○ happen   ○ sooner   ○ sudden

38 <u>s</u>ome

    ○ come   ○ each   ○ pass   ○ show

39 li<u>tt</u>le

    ○ caller   ○ mother   ○ father   ○ water

40 <u>f</u>ace

    ○ game   ○ stuff   ○ chat   ○ stick

STOP

itt Foresman 3

WRITING/GRAMMAR

DIRECTIONS

Read each passage. Some parts are underlined. The underlined parts may have mistakes in the way they are written or punctuated, or the words may need capital letters. Mark the space beside the best way to write each underlined part. If the underlined part needs no change, mark the choice "No mistake."

My brother and I went fishing yesterday. <u>Didn't catch a single</u>

(1)

<u>fish</u>. James said the water was too cold, but I think we used the

wrong bait. <u>Do fish eat gumdrops.</u>

(2)

---

1 ○ Not catching a single fish.
   ○ We didn't catch a single fish.
   ○ A single fish didn't catch.
   ○ No mistake

2 ○ Do fish eat gumdrops?
   ○ Do fish eat gumdrops!
   ○ Do fish eat gumdrops
   ○ No mistake

GO ON ➡

Marsha and Jane took the train to Boston. <u>Jane's mom too.</u> They
                                                      (3)

went to a museum and a baseball game. <u>Then they rode on the</u>
                                                      (4)

<u>on the swan boats.</u> For dinner, they had a picnic beside the

Charles River. <u>What a day they had?</u>
                        (5)

3   ○ Jane's mom too?
    ○ With Jane's mom too.
    ○ Jane's mom went too.
    ○ No mistake

4   ○ then they rode on the swan
      boats.
    ○ Then they rode on the swan
      boats.
    ○ Then rode on the swan
      boats.
    ○ No mistake

5   ○ What a day they had.
    ○ What a day they had!
    ○ What a day they had
    ○ No mistake

STOP

tt Foresman 3

WRITING

Think of something funny that happened to you when you were little. Write a story telling what happened and how you felt about it. Make sure your story has a beginning, middle, and end.

Prewriting Notes

_____

_____

_____

_____

_____

_____

_____

_____

_____

_____

_____

Foresman 3

GO ON

STOP

STUDY SKILLS

DIRECTIONS

Callie is writing a report on health. She looked in a textbook for information. Use the table of contents and index from the book to answer the questions.

CONTENTS

INDEX

1 Which chapter probably tells how many green vegetables a person should eat each day?
   ○ Chapter 1
   ○ Chapter 2
   ○ Chapter 3
   ○ Chapter 5

2 On which page does Chapter 4 begin?
   ○ page 15
   ○ page 22
   ○ page 36
   ○ page 44

GO ON

3 On which page or pages would Callie find information about how exercising helps a person lose fat?

○ page 22–27
○ page 28
○ page 29
○ pages 30–35

4 On which page or pages should Callie look to find out which type of doctor treats sore throats and ears?

○ page 38
○ pages 44–45
○ pages 46–48
○ pages 49

5 Callie wants to find the meaning of a word in this book. Where should she look?

○ in the table of contents
○ in the index
○ on the title page
○ in the glossary

Foresman 3

GO ON

Callie and her family live in Iowa. They are going on a trip. Callie looked at a map to see where they were going. Use the map to answer the questions.

6 What is the capital of Iowa?
○ Cedar Rapids
○ Sioux City
○ Des Moines
○ Lincoln

7 Where is Topeka located on the map?
○ 2-B
○ 5-C
○ 7-E
○ 5-D

GO ON

Foresman 3

8 Callie's family will drive from Sioux City, Iowa, to Scottsbluff, Nebraska. In which direction will they be traveling?

○ east
○ west
○ north
○ south

9 What is the capital of Missouri?

○ Kansas City
○ Springfield
○ Jefferson City
○ St. Louis

10 Where is Wichita, Kansas, located on the map?

○ 4-E
○ 6-F
○ 5-D
○ 8-E

The Whole Wide World

Name _____

Date _____

Scott Foresman
Reading
Grade 3

Editorial Offices
Glenview, Illinois • New York, New York

Sales Offices
Reading, Massachusetts • Duluth, Georgia • Glenview, Illinois
Carrollton, Texas • Menlo Park, California

ISBN 0-673-62423-4

3 4 5 6 7 8 9 10-EBA-06 05 04 03 02 01

READING: Comprehension

DIRECTIONS

Read each passage. Then read each question about the passage. Choose the best answer to each question. Mark the space for your answer.

A Garden Feast

Mrs. Squirrel was teaching her son Sam to gather food for himself in the woods. First she led him to a berry bush. "Take only the biggest berries. The small ones are hard and sour."

Sam found only four large berries. He popped them into his mouth and said, "I'm still hungry."

Mrs. Squirrel pointed to a small mushroom growing in the grass.

"Try that," she said.

Sam gobbled the mushroom. "I'm still hungry," he said.

Mrs. Squirrel had found a large nut. "Here, catch!" she said as she tossed it to Sam. He cracked the shell open with his teeth and quickly ate what was inside. "I'm still hungry," Sam complained, "and looking for bits of food here and there is hard work."

Rhonda Rabbit was just stirring from her nap under a tree. "I'm going to Farmer Javitt's garden," she told Sam. "Follow me there, and you'll have all the sweet corn you can eat."

With that, Rhonda hopped off toward the garden, and Sam followed close behind. They found a place to squeeze under the wire fence that enclosed the garden. Before long, they were nibbling on ears of yellow corn.

When Sam finally felt full, he gave Rhonda a thankful smile. "This is so much better than looking around for a nut here and a mushroom there," he said.

Just then a terrible banging sound made Sam jump with fear. "Let's get out of here!" shouted Rhonda. Sam and Rhonda squeezed back under the fence and hurried to the edge of the woods. Then they turned around and looked back at the garden. They saw Farmer Javitts standing among the corn stalks. In his hands he held a frying pan and a big metal spoon.

"The garden provides an easy meal, but it can be dangerous too," said Rhonda.

Sam's stomach hurt from running so fast after eating so much. He wondered if he should stick to gathering food in the woods.

tt Foresman 3

GO ON

1. In this story, the word <u>gobbled</u> means —
   - ○ planted.
   - ○ found.
   - ○ ate.
   - ○ picked.

2. Which part of this story could really happen?
   - ○ A rabbit and a squirrel are friends.
   - ○ A mother squirrel says, "Here, catch!"
   - ○ A farmer scares animals away from his garden.
   - ○ A rabbit talks to a squirrel.

3. The story says that Mrs. Squirrel <u>tossed</u> a nut to Sam. Which word means the same as <u>tossed</u>?
   - ○ threw
   - ○ sold
   - ○ cooked
   - ○ handed

4. What does Sam do in this story that a real squirrel could **not** do?
   - ○ He looks for food in the woods.
   - ○ He squeezes under a fence.
   - ○ He smiles at a rabbit.
   - ○ He runs away when he hears a loud noise.

5. The story says, "Rhonda Rabbit was just <u>stirring</u> from her nap." In this sentence, <u>stirring</u> means —
   - ○ mixing up.
   - ○ making a bed.
   - ○ feeling better.
   - ○ waking up.

Foresman 3

GO ON ▶

Too Much Trash

We Americans make a lot of trash and garbage. In fact, we create about four pounds of garbage per person every day. For some reason, Americans like to throw things away. We get rid of many things that could still be used. For example, we <u>discard</u> old clothing that could be worn by someone else.

We also throw away empty boxes, empty cans, and papers from school. What we throw away most often, though, is the packaging that our food comes in. It's true that we sometimes need this packaging to help keep our food clean and safe to eat. But often it is only there to make the food look better so we will buy it. Most of it ends up in the garbage.

What happens to all that garbage we throw away? These days, most of it gets buried in landfills, which are large holes that we dig in the ground. We fill them up with trash. Then we cover up the trash with dirt. This is a clean way to get rid of garbage, but someday we will run out of places for landfills. We need to start thinking about making less garbage, not more.

LANDFILL: Side View

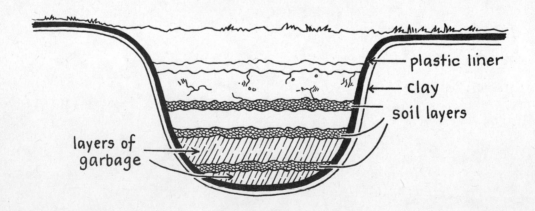

plastic liner
clay
soil layers

layers of garbage

GO ON

Foresman 3

6 What is the main idea of this passage?

- ○ Landfills are large holes in the ground.
- ○ Burying garbage takes up a lot of space.
- ○ Packaging keeps our food clean and safe to eat.
- ○ Americans throw away a lot of garbage and bury it in landfills.

7 What does the diagram on page 4 show?

- ○ how garbage is made
- ○ how landfills are built
- ○ how to use trash in new ways
- ○ how to package food

8 In a landfill, what is placed between layers of garbage?

- ○ soil
- ○ clay
- ○ plastic
- ○ grass

9 The selection says, "We discard old clothing that could be worn by someone else." The word discard means —

- ○ throw away.
- ○ invent.
- ○ repair or mend.
- ○ buy.

10 Which sentence supports the idea that Americans make a lot of garbage?

- ○ "We create about four pounds of garbage per person every day."
- ○ "We sometimes need this packaging to help keep our food clean."
- ○ "It is only there to make the food look better so we will buy it."
- ○ "Then we cover up the trash with dirt."

Volcanoes: Mountains of Fire

The word *volcano* comes from the name Vulcan. Vulcan was the Roman god of fire. The Romans believed he lived <u>beneath</u> an island near Italy. Sometimes the island spit out fire. The Romans called this island *Vulcano*.

A volcano is an opening in the earth through which lava, gas, and ash escape. Hot rock inside the earth is called magma. As the magma mixes with gas, it pushes upward. If it finds a weak spot in the surface of the earth, the magma breaks through. A volcano is born.

Once the magma reaches the outside, it is called lava. At first the lava is very hot. As it cools, it begins to form a hill or mountain around the opening where it came out. The mountain often has the shape of a cone. The lava flows down its sides, and hot lava destroys everything in its path.

Volcanoes are not all bad, though. They help build mountains and islands. Also, ash from a volcano helps make the soil rich. This helps plants grow better, and these plants then become food for other forms of life.

VOLCANO

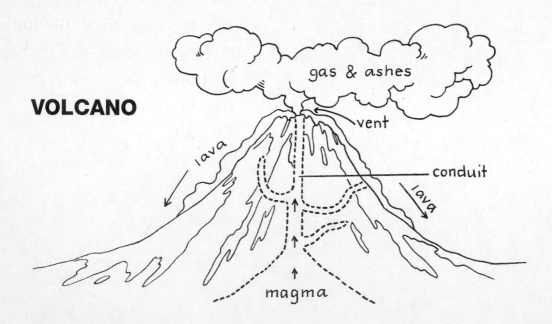

Foresman 3

11 What is this selection mostly about?

○ different kinds of volcanoes
○ the Roman god of fire
○ how volcanoes are formed
○ what is good about volcanoes

12 The selection says, "The Romans believed he lived <u>beneath</u> an island." Which word means the same as <u>beneath</u>?

○ under
○ around
○ between
○ either

13 Which sentence supports the idea that volcanoes are not all bad?

○ "Hot lava destroys everything in its path."
○ "The mountain often has the shape of a cone."
○ "Ash from a volcano helps make the soil rich."
○ "The word *volcano* comes from the name Vulcan."

14 Look at the diagram on page 6. Inside a volcano, magma moves upward through the —

○ lava.
○ conduit.
○ Vulcan.
○ island.

15 What is the opening at the top of the volcano called?

○ magma
○ vent
○ conduit
○ lava

t Foresman 3

Opening Night

Tracy could hardly wait for the play to begin. Her little brother Carl had an important part in the play. As Tracy walked into the hall with her mom and dad, a student gave her a program for the show.

The Third-Grade Class of Myers School Presents

The Fox and the Hound
Friday and Saturday, June 5 and 6, at 7:00 P.M.

Description
When they were little pups, Fox and Hound played together all the time. Then one day, Squirrel <u>warned</u> them that dogs hunt foxes. Squirrel said that a fox and a dog could not be friends. Fox and Hound laughed. They were not <u>worried</u>. But then Fox got caught in a hunter's trap. Maybe they should have listened to Squirrel . . .

Cast

Fox . . . . Gary Blake
Hound . . . . Ann Husk
Squirrel . . . . Carl Pinsky
Owl . . . . Megan Waring
Turtle . . . . Kim Shen
The Hunter . . . . Jon Danson

Cold drinks and other <u>refreshments</u> will be served after the play.

t Foresman 3

16 Which part of the play could **not** happen in real life?
- ○ A fox gets caught in a trap.
- ○ A squirrel talks to a dog.
- ○ A puppy likes to play.
- ○ A little fox plays every day.

17 The program says, "Squirrel <u>warned</u> them that dogs hunt foxes." Which word means the same as <u>warned</u>?
- ○ showed
- ○ trapped
- ○ proved
- ○ told

18 Which part of the play could really happen?
- ○ A fox laughs.
- ○ A dog laughs at a squirrel.
- ○ A fox gets caught in a trap.
- ○ A dog talks to a squirrel.

19 What are <u>refreshments</u>?
- ○ things to eat and drink
- ○ persons who act in a play
- ○ tickets for a show
- ○ people who watch a play

20 The program says, "They were not <u>worried</u>." Which word means the same as <u>worried</u>?
- ○ friendly
- ○ afraid
- ○ full-grown
- ○ together

STOP

Foresman 3

READING: Phonics

DIRECTIONS
Read the word. Find the word that has the same sound as the underlined letter or letters. Mark the space for your answer.

21 fa<u>c</u>e

○ can   ○ cliff   ○ less   ○ back

22 g<u>oo</u>d

○ rode   ○ could   ○ too   ○ out

23 n<u>ow</u>

○ house   ○ four   ○ slow   ○ would

24 <u>j</u>am

○ game   ○ rag   ○ page   ○ make

25 r<u>oo</u>m

○ come   ○ more   ○ rock   ○ boot

26 bu<u>s</u>

○ rice   ○ cub   ○ push   ○ much

GO ON

27 n<u>ou</u>n

  ○ know   ○ young   ○ court   ○ cow

28 t<u>ou</u>ch

  ○ count   ○ mouse   ○ should   ○ such

29 f<u>ou</u>nd

  ○ your   ○ hood   ○ gown   ○ root

30 t<u>oo</u>k

  ○ wood   ○ poke   ○ soon   ○ toad

31 <u>a</u>ge

  ○ gate   ○ bag   ○ egg   ○ jump

32 h<u>ow</u>

  ○ grow   ○ loud   ○ bowl   ○ hole

33 m<u>oo</u>n

  ○ tooth   ○ snow   ○ look   ○ moan

34 ni<u>c</u>e

  ○ chin   ○ neck   ○ boss   ○ can

35 s<u>ou</u>nd

  ○ slow   ○ you   ○ rough   ○ town

GO ON

DIRECTIONS
Read the underlined word. Choose the word that can be added to it to form a compound word. Mark the space for your answer.

36 <u>sun</u>
- ○ ray
- ○ shine
- ○ warm
- ○ bow

37 <u>cup</u>
- ○ milk
- ○ day
- ○ cake
- ○ spill

38 <u>play</u>
- ○ pen
- ○ boat
- ○ baby
- ○ one

39 <u>door</u>
- ○ car
- ○ stair
- ○ open
- ○ bell

40 <u>flash</u>
- ○ ball
- ○ town
- ○ light
- ○ red

STOP

tt Foresman 3

WRITING/GRAMMAR

DIRECTIONS

Read each story. Some parts are underlined. The underlined parts may have mistakes in the way they are written, or the words may need capital letters. Mark the space beside the best way to write each underlined part. If the underlined part needs no change, mark the choice "No mistake."

My friend David loves to visit New York. He thinks it is one of the

two best <u>city</u> in the United States. His other favorite place is
__(1)__

Chicago, because it is on <u>Lake michigan</u>. David loves to swim in
__(2)__

the lake.

---

1 ○ citys
   ○ cities
   ○ cityies
   ○ No mistake

2 ○ lake michigan
   ○ lake Michigan
   ○ Lake Michigan
   ○ No mistake

GO ON ➤

Cora got a letter from Darlene today. Darlene lives on a ranch

near <u>casper, wyoming</u>. All of the <u>children</u> in her school had to
       (3)   **(4)**

write letters to people in other states. <u>Darlenes'</u> teacher wanted to
                                       (5)

see if the class could get letters back from at least thirty different

states.

3 ◯ Casper, Wyoming
   ◯ casper, Wyoming
   ◯ Casper, wyoming
   ◯ No mistake

4 ◯ childs
   ◯ childrens'
   ◯ children's
   ◯ No mistake

5 ◯ Darlenes
   ◯ Darlenes's
   ◯ Darlene's
   ◯ No mistake

STOP

tt Foresman 3

WRITING

Think about a place in or near your home where you like to go. It might be a room, a yard, a park, or another kind of place.

Write a description of the place. Tell what it looks like and what you can see there. Include words that describe shapes and colors.

Prewriting Notes

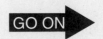
GO ON

STOP

STUDY SKILLS

DIRECTIONS

Use the part of the dictionary page below to answer the questions on the next page. Choose the best answer to each question. Mark the space beside your answer.

yap (yap), **1** a quick, sharp bark; yelp. **2** to bark in a quick, sharp way; yelp: *The little dog yapped at me.* 1 *noun,* 2 *verb,* **yaps, yapped, yap·ping.**

yard[1] (yärd), **1** a piece of ground near or around a house, barn, school, or other building: *You can play outside, but you must not leave the yard.* **2** a piece of enclosed ground for some special purpose or business: *a chicken yard.* **3** a space with many tracks where railroad cars are stored, shifted around, serviced, or made up into new trains: *My dad works in the railroad yards.* *noun.*

yard[2] (yärd), **1** a unit of length equal to 36 inches; 3 feet: *I bought three yards of blue cloth for curtains.* **2** a beam or pole fastened across a mast and used to support a sail. *noun.*

yard·stick (yärd/stik/), a stick one yard long, used for measuring. *noun.*

yarn (yärn), **1** any spun thread, especially that prepared for weaving or knitting: *I'm knitting a scarf from this yarn.* **2** a tale; story: *The old sailor made up his yarns as he told them.* *noun.*

yawn (yȯn), **1** to open the mouth wide because one is sleepy, tired, or bored. **2** the act of opening the mouth in this way. **3** to open wide: *The canyon yawned in front of us.* 1,3 *verb,* 2 *noun.*

yd., yard. *plural* **yd.** or **yds.**

ye (yē), an old word meaning **you.** *If ye are thirsty, drink. pronoun.*

yea (yā), **1** yes. **2** indeed. **3** a vote or voter in favor of something: *The yeas outnumber the nays, so the plan is approved.* 1,2 *adverb,* 3 *noun.*

a hat	i it	oi oil	ch child	⎧ a in about
ā age	ī ice	ou out	ng long	⎪ e in taken
ä far	o hot	u cup	sh she	ə = ⎨ i in pencil
e let	ō open	ů put	th thin	⎪ o in lemon
ē equal	ȯ saw	ü rule	ᵀн then	⎩ u in circus
ėr term	ô order		zh measure	

yel·low (yel/ō), **1** the color of gold, butter, or ripe lemons. **2** having this color. **3** to make or become yellow: *Paper yellows with age.* **4** the yolk of an egg. **5** cowardly. 1,4 *noun,* 2,5 *adjective,* 3 *verb.*

yellow fever, a dangerous, infectious disease of warm climates that causes high fever and turns the skin yellow. It is transmitted by the bite of a certain kind of mosquito. Yellow fever was once common in some southern parts of the United States.

yel·low·ish (yel/ō ish), somewhat yellow. *adjective.*

yellow jacket, a wasp marked with bright yellow.

Yellow Pages, a telephone book or section of a telephone book that is printed on yellow paper and lists businesses and professional people. The kinds of business are listed alphabetically, and so are the names within each kind.

yelp (yelp), **1** the quick, sharp bark or cry of a dog or fox. **2** to make such a bark or cry. 1 *noun,* 2 *verb.*

Yem·en (yem/ən), a country in Arabia, in southwestern Asia. *noun.*

yen (yen), the unit of money in Japan. *noun, plural* **yen.**

t Foresman 3

GO ON

1 What is a <u>yen</u>?
- ○ a vote in favor of something
- ○ a country in Arabia
- ○ the unit of money in Japan
- ○ a telephone book

2 The <u>ea</u> in <u>yea</u> is pronounced like the —
- ○ <u>a</u> in <u>age</u>.
- ○ <u>a</u> in <u>hat</u>.
- ○ <u>e</u> in <u>let</u>.
- ○ <u>e</u> in <u>equal</u>.

3 What does <u>yard</u> mean in this sentence?
The train pulled into the <u>yard</u> for repairs.
- ○ a piece of ground near a house
- ○ a unit of length equal to 36 inches
- ○ a beam or pole fastened across a mast
- ○ a place where railroad cars are stored

4 Look at the guide words on the dictionary page. Which of these words could also be on this same dictionary page?
- ○ yew
- ○ yak
- ○ young
- ○ yule

5 What does <u>yellow</u> mean in this sentence?
The floor began to <u>yellow</u> from the effects of the sun.
- ○ the color of butter
- ○ the yolk of an egg
- ○ cowardly
- ○ to make or become yellow

GO ON ▶

DIRECTIONS

Choose the best answer to each question about alphabetical order.
Mark the space beside your answer.

6 Which word comes **first** in alphabetical order?
- ○ coat
- ○ cross
- ○ cure
- ○ climb

7 Which word comes **first** in alphabetical order?
- ○ journey
- ○ jolt
- ○ join
- ○ joust

8 Which word comes before <u>skip</u> in alphabetical order?
- ○ sting
- ○ shake
- ○ slow
- ○ spark

9 Which word comes **last** in alphabetical order?
- ○ moon
- ○ mold
- ○ mouth
- ○ monkey

10 Which word comes **last** in alphabetical order?
- ○ thinking
- ○ thunder
- ○ through
- ○ thought

STOP

tt Foresman 3

Getting the Job Done

Name _____

Date _____

Scott Foresman

Reading

Grade 3

Editorial Offices
Glenview, Illinois • New York, New York

Sales Offices
Reading, Massachusetts • Duluth, Georgia • Glenview, Illinois
Carrollton, Texas • Menlo Park, California

ISBN 0-673-62424-2

3 4 5 6 7 8 9 10-EBA-06 05 04 03 02 01

READING: Comprehension

DIRECTIONS
Read each passage. Then read each question about the passage. Choose the best answer to each question. Mark the space for your answer.

The Farmer and the Forest Animals

Long ago a farmer moved to the middle of a forest. Right away, the farmer started getting ready for planting. First he cut down trees. Next he rolled rocks out of the way. Then he started digging holes around his field.

The forest animals watched the farmer work. "He must be digging holes for seeds!" Skunk said. Like the others, Skunk was looking forward to eating the crops the farmer would plant.

Then Deer said, "Look! He is not planting seeds. He is putting up fence posts! The farmer is building a fence to keep us out!"

Deer was <u>right</u>. Before long, the farmer had built a tall fence around his field. Then he plowed and planted seeds. Soon crops began to grow. The farmer was satisfied with the job he had done.

Then things went wrong for the farmer. The summer turned hot and dry. Hardly any rain fell. The crops

turned brown. Each day, the farmer walked his field, shaking his head with worry. When fall finally came, the farmer had no crops to pick and no food for the winter.

The forest animals knew the farmer was in trouble. "It serves him right," said Skunk, "for keeping us away."

"Even so, we must help him," said Deer. The other animals agreed. Together they gathered berries and nuts from the forest. One night, while the farmer slept, they left the food at his door.

The next morning, the animals awoke to see the farmer taking down his fence. When the last post lay on the ground, the farmer turned toward the forest. "Thank you for your kindness, dear animals," he called. "I have no food to share with you now, but next spring I will plant again. Then, what is mine will be yours too."

From that time on, the farmer and the forest animals lived happily together.

t Foresman 3

1 What step did the farmer take first to get ready for planting?
- ◯ digging holes
- ◯ putting up a fence
- ◯ cutting down trees
- ◯ rolling rocks away

2 The story says, "Deer was right." What does right mean in this sentence?
- ◯ correct
- ◯ well or healthy
- ◯ at once
- ◯ opposite of left

3 Which sentence from the story helps you picture in your mind how the farmer's field looked?
- ◯ "Then things went wrong for the farmer."
- ◯ "The other animals agreed."
- ◯ "The crops turned brown."
- ◯ "The forest animals knew the farmer was in trouble."

4 What did the farmer do after he found the food at his door?
- ◯ He picked his crops.
- ◯ He took down his fence.
- ◯ He planted seeds.
- ◯ He gave food to the animals.

5 Which is the best summary of this story?
- ◯ A farmer moved to the middle of a forest. The forest animals did not care about him.
- ◯ A farmer built a fence around his field. Then he planted crops and watched them grow.
- ◯ One summer there was hardly any rain. The farmer and the forest animals had little food.
- ◯ A farmer built a fence to keep animals out, but his crops did not grow. The animals gave him food, so he took the fence down.

GO ON

Foresman 3

Puddles

Rain has fallen all day long,
Making puddles deep and wide.
Now Hobo is at the door,
Whining to go outside.

"Go, boy!" I call as I let him out.
He takes off like a flash.
He heads for the biggest puddle of all
And flops in with a splash.

Soon Hobo races back to the house,
Muddy from nose to tail.
"Clean that dog up!" my mother yells.
She hands me a brush and a pail.

So I fill the pail and add some soap.
I scrub and rinse and scrub some more.
But Hobo decides he's had enough,
And shakes himself off on the floor.

Then Hobo curls up in his favorite <u>spot</u>.
Before long he falls asleep,
And I'm almost certain he's dreaming
Of puddles, wide and deep.

Foresman 3

GO ON

6 What does Hobo do first when he goes outside?
- ◯ falls asleep
- ◯ stands at the door
- ◯ shakes himself off
- ◯ flops into a puddle

7 What did Hobo look like as he raced back to the house?
- ◯ He was dripping with mud.
- ◯ He was tired and worn out.
- ◯ He was hot and panting.
- ◯ He was covered with soap suds.

8 What is the first step the child in this poem takes to clean Hobo?
- ◯ drying Hobo off
- ◯ putting water and soap in a pail
- ◯ scrubbing and rinsing Hobo
- ◯ brushing Hobo's fur

9 The poem says, "Then Hobo curls up in his favorite <u>spot</u>." What does <u>spot</u> mean in this sentence?
- ◯ ready or on hand
- ◯ a stain
- ◯ to find or pick out
- ◯ a place

10 Which is the best summary of this poem?
- ◯ Hobo runs outside. Then he comes in and falls asleep.
- ◯ Hobo plays in a puddle. After getting cleaned up, he sleeps and dreams about puddles.
- ◯ Hobo whines at the door. Then he runs outside and sees a puddle.
- ◯ Hobo gets scrubbed and rinsed. Then he has a dream about puddles.

GO ON ▶

The Skating Lesson

Kasha sat on the bench and pulled on her new skates. Just then a picture popped into her head. Dressed in a fancy costume, she was gliding across the ice before a cheering crowd. "I *will* be a great skater someday," Kasha said. Then she slowly stood up and stepped onto the rink. Suddenly Kasha's feet flew out from under her, and she landed flat on her back on the ice.

"Easy does it, Kasha," said a friendly voice. Kasha looked up to see her neighbor, Ms. Reid, holding out her hands. Kasha took them and pulled herself up.

"I'm trying to teach myself to skate," Kasha explained, "but it's harder than I thought. Those skaters on TV make it look so easy!"

Ms. Reid nodded. "That's because they've had years of lessons," she said. "I used to take lessons myself. Let me give you a few <u>tips</u>."

Ms. Reid knew what she was doing. First she taught Kasha to keep her knees bent. Next she showed her how to move her skates. "Glide, don't step," she said over and over until Kasha got it right. Then she showed Kasha how to move her arms. "Swing them back and forth, just like when you run," said Ms. Reid.

Before long, Kasha had put it all together. She skated slowly, but her feet and arms moved smoothly. Soon she felt relaxed enough to smile as she glided along.

"You learn fast, Kasha," said Ms. Reid. "Keep it up, and soon you'll be ready for spins."

"Jumps too?" asked Kasha.

Ms. Reid laughed. "Those come later," she said, "but you'll get there if you try hard enough."

"Oh, I will try hard!" said Kasha. Then she pushed off for a slow, steady glide across the ice.

Foresman 3

GO ON

11 What happened right after Kasha stepped onto the ice?

○ She put on her skates.
○ A crowd began to cheer.
○ She saw Ms. Reid.
○ Her feet flew out from under her.

12 Ms. Reid says, "Let me give you a few tips." What does tips mean in this sentence?

○ upsets or turns over
○ useful hints
○ end parts
○ small gifts of money

13 The first thing Kasha had to learn about skating was to —

○ swing her arms.
○ spin around.
○ keep her knees bent.
○ jump into the air.

14 Which words help you visualize how Kasha looked as she skated at the end of the story?

○ "She pushed off for a slow, steady glide across the ice."
○ "Soon you'll be ready for spins."
○ "You'll get there if you try hard enough."
○ "You learn fast, Kasha."

15 Which is the best summary of this story?

○ Kasha had trouble skating until Ms. Reid gave her a lesson. Then she learned fast.
○ Ms. Reid is Kasha's neighbor. She saw Kasha at the skating rink.
○ Kasha watched skaters on TV. She tried to skate as well as they did, but she was not able to do it.
○ Ms. Reid is a good skater, but Kasha is better.

GO ON ➡

Which Shirt Should You Choose?

The Tigers baseball team is buying uniforms, and the coach must choose between white or black shirts. Which color will keep you cooler on hot summer afternoons? This experiment will tell you the answer.

What you need:
a sheet of white paper
a sheet of black paper
2 thermometers
a watch

What you do:
1. On a sunny day, lay both sheets of paper on the ground.
2. <u>Place</u> a thermometer under each sheet.
3. Wait ten minutes.
4. Read each thermometer. Which one has the higher temperature?

What happens and why:
The thermometer under the black paper will show a higher temperature than the one under the white paper. Why? A white surface reflects light, so most of the sun's rays bounced off the white paper. Black absorbs, or takes in, light, so the black paper got warmer than the white paper.

Now you know why a white jersey will feel cooler than a black one on a hot summer afternoon.

Foresman 3

16 What is the last step in this experiment?

○ finding thermometers and a watch

○ waiting ten minutes

○ laying sheets of paper on the ground

○ reading each thermometer

17 The directions say, "Place a thermometer under each sheet." What does place mean in this sentence?

○ to put in a certain spot

○ a duty or job

○ a person's space or seat

○ to finish second in a race

18 If you leave the black paper in the sun, what happens next?

○ It gets smaller.

○ It turns white.

○ It gets warmer.

○ It gets wet.

19 Picture yourself as a player on this baseball team after doing this experiment. What are you wearing?

○ a white shirt

○ a red cap

○ black socks

○ gray shorts

20 Which is the best summary of this passage?

○ Do an experiment before you decide to join a baseball team.

○ Use thermometers and paper to find out if a white shirt is cooler than a black one.

○ Paper might reflect light, or it might absorb it.

○ Your baseball team wants to keep cool on hot summer afternoons.

STOP

t Foresman 3

READING: Phonics

DIRECTIONS
Read the word. Find the word that has the same sound as the underlined letter or letters. Mark the space for your answer.

21 n<u>ear</u>
  ○ were   ○ tar   ○ here   ○ farm

22 st<u>ar</u>
  ○ mark   ○ care   ○ dear   ○ pair

23 b<u>are</u>
  ○ fear   ○ hard   ○ fair   ○ born

24 h<u>ear</u>t
  ○ ear   ○ rent   ○ deer   ○ jar

25 <u>r</u>oad
  ○ wait   ○ when   ○ wrap   ○ white

26 <u>n</u>ew
  ○ kiss   ○ wet   ○ soggy   ○ knot

t Foresman 3

27 rai<u>n</u>

   ○ page   ○ grip   ○ sign   ○ wig

28 ca<u>m</u>e

   ○ lamb   ○ fall   ○ done   ○ rub

29 tele<u>ph</u>one

   ○ happen   ○ mother   ○ copy   ○ before

30 tea<u>ch</u>es

   ○ pitcher   ○ baker   ○ known   ○ races

31 da<u>sh</u>es

   ○ scared   ○ castle   ○ mushy   ○ slipper

32 ga<u>th</u>er

   ○ trick   ○ return   ○ softer   ○ other

GO ON

t Foresman 3

DIRECTIONS
Choose the base word of the underlined word. Mark the space for your answer.

33 <u>unkindly</u>
⟶ ○ kind   ○ unkind   ○ kin   ○ kindly

34 <u>flowering</u>
○ lower   ○ low   ○ ring   ○ flower

35 <u>distrustful</u>
○ dis   ○ trust   ○ rust   ○ trustful

36 <u>golden</u>
○ old   ○ den   ○ gold   ○ olden

GO ON ▶

DIRECTIONS

Add the suffix to the base word. Choose the correct spelling of the new word. Mark the space for your answer.

37 mystery + -ous =
- ○ mysterous
- ○ mysteryous
- ○ mysterious
- ○ mysteryious

38 beauty + -ful =
- ○ beautyful
- ○ beautiful
- ○ beautful
- ○ beautyiful

39 sure + -ly =
- ○ surely
- ○ surly
- ○ surily
- ○ sureily

40 silly + -ness =
- ○ sillyness
- ○ sillness
- ○ sillyiness
- ○ silliness

STOP

WRITING/GRAMMAR

DIRECTIONS

Read the passage. Choose the word or words that best fit in each numbered blank. Mark the space for your answer.

There is a new boy in Heidi's class. His name _____ Galeno.
(1)

Heidi wants to make friends with Galeno. Yesterday she _____
(2)

her snack with him. Galeno _____ the dried banana chips. He
(3)

_____ they were delicious. Tomorrow Galeno _____ a special
(4)   (5)

snack for Heidi.

---

1. ○ were
   ○ is
   ○ are
   ○ being

2. ○ will share
   ○ shares
   ○ is sharing
   ○ shared

3. ○ tasted
   ○ tastes
   ○ will taste
   ○ tasting

4. ○ think
   ○ thoughted
   ○ thinked
   ○ thought

5. ○ brought
   ○ will bring
   ○ bring
   ○ was bringing

STOP

Foresman 3

WRITING

Think about two different jobs you might like to have when you are a grown-up. Write a paragraph that tells how the jobs are alike and how they are different.

Prewriting Notes

GO ON ➡

_____

_____

_____

_____

_____

_____

_____

_____

_____

_____

_____

STOP

STUDY SKILLS

DIRECTIONS

Cody is writing a report about outer space. He begins by looking for information in an encyclopedia. Use the set of encyclopedias shown below to answer the questions.

A-B	C	D	E-F	G·H	I	J-K	L-M	N	O·P	Q-R	S	T	U-V	W·X·Y·Z
VOL 1	VOL 2	VOL 3	VOL 4	VOL 5	VOL 6	VOL 7	VOL 8	VOL 9	VOL 10	VOL 11	VOL 12	VOL 13	VOL 14	VOL 15

1 In which volume should Cody look to find information about Saturn?
- ○ Vol. 1
- ○ Vol. 4
- ○ Vol. 12
- ○ Vol. 13

2 In which volume should Cody look for information about the Hubble telescope?
- ○ Vol. 5
- ○ Vol. 8
- ○ Vol. 10
- ○ Vol. 14

GO ON ➤

Foresman 3

3 In which volume should Cody look for information on the Apollo space missions?
- ○ Vol. 1
- ○ Vol. 8
- ○ Vol. 13
- ○ Vol. 15

4 In Volume 2, Cody should look for an entry about comets on a page with which guide words?
- ○ **cold — color**
- ○ **comedy — comma**
- ○ **concert — Congress**
- ○ **copper — coral**

5 In Volume 10, Cody should look for an entry about Pluto on a page with which guide words?
- ○ **painting — palace**
- ○ **pike — pilot**
- ○ **plastic — play**
- ○ **plum — Plymouth**

t Foresman 3

DIRECTIONS

Choose the best answer to each question about reference sources that Cody can use to find information for his report.

6 To find information about the outer space exhibit that is about to open at the science museum, Cody should look in —
- ○ a newspaper.
- ○ an atlas.
- ○ an encyclopedia.
- ○ a dictionary.

7 To find a map that shows Cape Canaveral, Florida, where space shuttles take off, Cody should look in —
- ○ an almanac.
- ○ a dictionary.
- ○ an atlas.
- ○ a newspaper.

8 To find out why the planet Saturn has rings, Cody should look in —
- ○ a newspaper.
- ○ an atlas.
- ○ a dictionary.
- ○ an encyclopedia.

9 To find the meaning of the word gravity, Cody should look in —
- ○ a dictionary.
- ○ a newspaper.
- ○ an atlas.
- ○ an almanac.

10 To find a list of space flights that took place last year, Cody should look in —
- ○ a telephone directory.
- ○ an almanac.
- ○ an atlas.
- ○ a dictionary.

STOP

t Foresman 3

From Past to Present

Name _____

Date _____

Scott Foresman
Reading
Grade 3

Editorial Offices
Glenview, Illinois • New York, New York

Sales Offices
Reading, Massachusetts • Duluth, Georgia • Glenview, Illinois
Carrollton, Texas • Menlo Park, California

ISBN 0-673-62425-0

3 4 5 6 7 8 9 10-EBA-06 05 04 03 02 01

READING: Comprehension

DIRECTIONS

Read each passage. Then read each question about the passage. Choose the best answer to each question. Mark the space for your answer.

The Bear and the Apple Tree

One summer day, a bear came upon an apple tree in the middle of a meadow. The bear was happy, for apples were his favorite food, but he knew better than to eat the fruit right away. "Now these apples are small, green, and <u>tart</u>," he said. "I will not touch them until fall when they are large, red, and sweet. What a feast that will be!"

As the summer passed, the bear often stopped by the apple tree.

Each time, he was excited to see how ripe the apples were growing, and each time he resisted eating even one. The bear was proud of himself for being so patient. "Yes, I would enjoy a young, pink apple today," the bear told himself. "But I will bide my time until it is ripe. It will taste so much better then."

Before long, fall arrived. The days grew shorter and cooler. The leaves changed color. Now when the bear stopped by the tree, he

saw that the apples were large, red, and ripe. The bear's mouth watered, and he reached up to pick an apple. Then suddenly he stopped himself. "I have waited all this time," the bear said, "so surely I can wait just one more day. One more day will make the apples even sweeter."

That night, asleep in his cave, the bear dreamed about the sweet apples he would eat the next day.

But morning brought bad news for the bear. When he stepped out of his cave, he saw that the ground and trees were covered with frost.

"Oh, no, my apples!" shouted the bear. He hurried to the apple tree. When he got there, the bear nearly cried. Covered with frost, the apples had shriveled and turned brown. Not a single one was fit to eat.

1 Which is one of the big ideas or themes in this story?
- ○ You can always tell what the weather will be.
- ○ Fruit is good for you.
- ○ A plan that seems wise can go wrong.
- ○ Time can seem to pass slowly.

2 Where does most of this story take place?
- ○ in a cave
- ○ on a mountain
- ○ in a meadow
- ○ in a house

3 The story says, "Now these apples are small, green, and tart." Which word means the opposite of tart?
- ○ pink
- ○ sweet
- ○ large
- ○ young

4 At the end of this story, the season is —
- ○ winter.
- ○ spring.
- ○ summer.
- ○ fall.

5 What lesson did the bear learn in this story?
- ○ If you wait too long, you may lose the thing you want.
- ○ Everyone has troubles.
- ○ Don't take a good thing when you can have the best.
- ○ Hard work pays off.

6 What kind of story is this?
- ○ a fable
- ○ realistic fiction
- ○ a mystery
- ○ science fiction

Tornado Warning

Hank was rolling up his sleeping bag when a car pulled into the Gibsons' driveway. "It's your mother, Hank," called Mrs. Gibson. "She's a little early, isn't she? I'm just making breakfast."

Hank looked at Jordy. "Something must be wrong," he said. "She wasn't supposed to pick me up until this afternoon."

Hank and Jordy hurried downstairs. Then they heard Mrs. Gibson laughing. "Goodness, Gloria, we're in the mountains of New York. We don't have tornadoes here!"

"I hope you're right, Anna," Hank's mother answered. "But there was a tornado warning on the TV. When I was growing up in Oklahoma, we learned to take a tornado warning seriously."

"Nothing's going to happen," said Hank. "Please let me stay."

"No, I'm sorry," Hank's mother said. "I'm taking you home."

Hank and his mother drove home in silence. Finally she said, "Mrs. Gibson thinks I'm silly, but if there's a tornado, I want you home where I know you are safe. That's the <u>sensible</u> thing to do."

The sky was darkening when Hank and his mother got home. Before long, rain began falling, with rumbles of thunder and flashes of lightning. Hank was watching from a window. "Mom!" he cried. "Look at the trees! The winds are bending them right over! Is this a tornado?"

Before his mother could answer, the telephone rang. "Yes, Anna, that's what's happening here too," she said. Then she added, "The basement is the safest place. Stay there until the winds die down. I'll call you back then."

Hearing his mother's instructions, Hank grabbed a flashlight and went downstairs to the basement. His mother hung up the phone and followed him down. She put a hand on Hank's shoulder and said, "We'll be fine here, son." Hank nodded. He was glad to be home.

t Foresman 3

7 What is the theme of this story?

- ○ Don't be afraid of danger.
- ○ A friend won't let you down.
- ○ Keep your ideas to yourself.
- ○ It is better to be safe than sorry.

8 Around what time of day does this story begin?

- ○ early morning
- ○ noon
- ○ late afternoon
- ○ evening

9 Hank's mother went to the Gibsons' house because —

- ○ Hank wanted to leave.
- ○ she was taking the boys to school.
- ○ Mrs. Gibson invited her to breakfast.
- ○ she wanted to take Hank home.

10 In the story, Hank's mother says, "That's the <u>sensible</u> thing to do." Which word means the opposite of <u>sensible</u>?

- ○ foolish
- ○ early
- ○ right
- ○ glad

11 Where are Hank and his mother when the story ends?

- ○ at the Gibsons' house
- ○ in their car
- ○ at the school
- ○ in their basement

12 What lesson does Mrs. Gibson learn in this story?

- ○ Take advice from someone who knows more than you.
- ○ Make as many friends as you can.
- ○ You are probably right more often than you are wrong.
- ○ Don't let other people tell you what to do.

t Foresman 3

From Mexico to Massachusetts

Last night, Papa asked me if I like living in the United States now. To my surprise, I realized my answer was yes. Not so long ago, I did not like it here at all. My name is Alicia Hernandez, and I am nine years old. I have lived in Boston, Massachusetts, for two years. Before that I lived in Mexico City, Mexico. We came to Boston because Papa, who is a doctor, wanted to learn some new skills by working at a big hospital here. The day he announced his plan to Mama, my brothers, and me, I was upset. "You are already a good doctor," I told him. "You know enough already."

Though I believed what I said, I really was being selfish. I knew that moving to Boston would mean leaving my home, friends, and everything familiar. "Boston will be awful!" I told Papa.

Boston did seem <u>awful</u> at first, and I think even Papa agreed. Our new house was on a street where no one else spoke Spanish. Most of my classmates didn't either, so I felt lonely at school. Mama had trouble cooking our favorite Mexican dishes because she could not buy the ingredients at the supermarket. We celebrated Mexican holidays alone because no one else knew about them. But the winter weather bothered me most of all. I hated wearing boots and mittens and having recess on a cold, snowy playground.

In time, though, life in Boston has gotten better. I have learned to speak English and have made some good friends. Mama has found a Mexican market so she can make our favorite dishes. Even better, I have taken a fancy to many American foods. We have also made Mexican American friends, so we celebrate our holidays with them. Best of all, I look forward to snowy days, when my brothers and I can go sledding and build snow forts.

Papa says we will probably return to Mexico City next year. I think I will be glad to go home, but I also know I will miss Boston.

t Foresman 3

13 The story says, "Boston did seem <u>awful</u>." Which word means the opposite of <u>awful</u>?
- ◯ lonely
- ◯ wonderful
- ◯ cold
- ◯ terrible

14 Why did Papa move with his family to Boston?
- ◯ He had friends there.
- ◯ He thought it was a great place to live.
- ◯ He was tired of Mexico City.
- ◯ He wanted to work in a hospital there.

15 How was Alicia's life different when she first moved to Boston?
- ◯ She stopped going to school.
- ◯ She did not have neighbors who spoke Spanish.
- ◯ She hardly ever saw her father.
- ◯ She did not celebrate Mexican holidays.

16 How is Mexico City different from Boston?
- ◯ It has fewer people.
- ◯ It has warmer winters.
- ◯ It is smaller.
- ◯ It has more hospitals.

17 Which sentence from the story contains an idiom?
- ◯ "I have taken a fancy to many American foods."
- ◯ "Life in Boston has gotten better."
- ◯ "I felt lonely at school."
- ◯ "Mama has found a Mexican market."

18 What kind of story is this?
- ◯ historical fiction
- ◯ folk tale
- ◯ myth
- ◯ autobiography

GO ON

ott Foresman 3

What Happened When Benny Went Shopping?

Dear Mr. Perkins:

As the owner of Perkins Department Store, you must hope that your clerks always help your customers. You should know that some do, but some don't.

I went to your store last week to buy a present for my aunt, since Perkins has always been her favorite place to shop. I had nine dollars to spend. First I went to the perfume counter. The clerk there ignored me until I asked her to help me pick out a perfume for my aunt. When I told her how much money I had, she laughed. Then she said, "About all you can afford in this store is a pair of socks."

I felt terrible. I decided to go to another store, so I headed for the exit. Just then a different clerk noticed me and asked if he could help. I told him no, since I did not have enough money to buy anything my aunt would like. Then the clerk asked if my aunt likes flowers. When I said yes, he led me to the gardening department and helped me put together a great gift.

What was it? For about eight dollars, I bought a clay pot, some potting soil, and six tulip bulbs. I brought everything home, filled the pot with soil, and planted the bulbs. Then I gave the gift to my aunt. She loved it! She put the pot in a sunny window. In a few weeks, she'll have a pot of tulips to <u>brighten</u> her house.

By the way, the clerk who helped me is named Mr. Norton. He really went out of his way to help, and I'm grateful. In my opinion, the clerk at the perfume counter should take a lesson from him.

Sincerely yours,

Benny Newman

tt Foresman 3

19 Benny went to Perkins Department Store to —
- ◯ meet Mr. Norton.
- ◯ buy some socks.
- ◯ learn a lesson from a clerk.
- ◯ buy a present for his aunt.

20 The letter says the tulips will <u>brighten</u> the house. Which word means the opposite of <u>brighten</u>?
- ◯ fill
- ◯ clean
- ◯ darken
- ◯ improve

21 How were the socks and the tulips alike?
- ◯ Benny's aunt wanted them both.
- ◯ Both cost less than nine dollars.
- ◯ Mr. Norton said both were good presents.
- ◯ Both were sold at the perfume counter.

22 The letter says, "He really went out of his way to help." What does this mean?
- ◯ He tried hard.
- ◯ He went the wrong way.
- ◯ He got lost.
- ◯ He looked the other way.

23 How was the first clerk different from Mr. Norton?
- ◯ She worked hard.
- ◯ She was funny.
- ◯ She had good ideas.
- ◯ She was rude.

24 Benny wrote this letter because he wanted to —
- ◯ say how much he likes shopping.
- ◯ tell Mr. Perkins about the two clerks he met.
- ◯ complain about high prices.
- ◯ tell Mr. Perkins how to plant tulips.

tt Foresman 3

STOP

READING: Phonics

DIRECTIONS

Read the word. Find the word that has the same sound as the underlined letter or letters. Mark the space for your answer.

25 c<u>oi</u>n
- ○ young
- ○ lion
- ○ moon
- ○ toys

26 l<u>oy</u>al
- ○ point
- ○ could
- ○ boot
- ○ float

27 n<u>oi</u>sy
- ○ almost
- ○ enjoy
- ○ dollar
- ○ foolish

28 ann<u>oy</u>
- ○ flower
- ○ cookie
- ○ become
- ○ voice

29 p<u>ou</u>r
- ○ burn
- ○ tore
- ○ pear
- ○ word

30 thi<u>r</u>d
- ○ learn
- ○ fire
- ○ their
- ○ heart

GO ON →

tt Foresman 3

31 c<u>or</u>n

○ hour   ○ card   ○ year   ○ four

32 h<u>ur</u>t

○ fear   ○ were   ○ your   ○ dare

33 <u>sk</u>ip

○ spike   ○ slip   ○ sick   ○ skate

34 ha<u>nd</u>

○ need   ○ done   ○ wind   ○ pants

35 <u>cr</u>isp

○ chore   ○ reach   ○ clear   ○ crown

36 da<u>mp</u>

○ jump   ○ snap   ○ mop   ○ poem

Foresman 3

37 <u>squ</u>eak

  ◯ skill   ◯ square   ◯ sunk   ◯ quits

38 <u>scr</u>ub

  ◯ scout   ◯ scrape   ◯ crib   ◯ stork

39 <u>thr</u>one

  ◯ three   ◯ though   ◯ there   ◯ thick

40 <u>str</u>ange

  ◯ traps   ◯ string   ◯ skirt   ◯ stand

GO ON ▶

t Foresman 3

DIRECTIONS

Read each pair of sentences. Choose the correct form of the word to fit the blank. Mark the space for your answer.

41 Mr. Herbert has a new dog. The _____ fur is long and shaggy.
- ○ dogs
- ○ dog's
- ○ dog
- ○ dogs'

42 The girls in our family share a bedroom. The _____ room is down the hall.
- ○ girl
- ○ girl's
- ○ girls
- ○ girls'

43 This is my winter coat. My _____ zipper needs to be fixed.
- ○ coat's
- ○ coates
- ○ coats'
- ○ coats

44 Three friends are riding a train together. The _____ trip will take six hours.
- ○ friends
- ○ friends'
- ○ friend
- ○ friend's

45 Ms. Lyons had her car fixed. The _____ tires had to be replaced.
- ○ cares
- ○ cars
- ○ car's
- ○ cars'

STOP

Foresman 3

WRITING/GRAMMAR

DIRECTIONS

Read the passage. Choose the word or words that best fit in each numbered blank. Mark the space for your answer.

Getting up in the morning is hard for Wendy. She bought the _____
(1)
alarm clock she could find, but it _____ wake her up. The alarm
(2)
bothers Wendy's dog, though. He licks her on _____ sides of her face
(3)
until she turns it off. Wendy gets going slowly, but she moves much

_____ when she hears the school bus head north on _____. She
(4)   (5)
knows the bus will be back to pick her up in a few minutes.

1 ○ most louder
   ○ loudest
   ○ loud
   ○ more loudly

2 ○ does'nt
   ○ doesnt'
   ○ doesnt
   ○ doesn't

3 ○ the
   ○ a
   ○ these
   ○ an

4 ○ fast
   ○ most faster
   ○ more fastest
   ○ faster

5 ○ center street
   ○ Center street
   ○ Center Street
   ○ center Street

STOP

t Foresman 3

WRITING

Think of a favorite snack that you have learned to prepare for yourself. Write a how-to report telling how to make this snack. Write the steps so that they are in the right order and are easy to understand.

Prewriting Notes

STOP

STUDY SKILLS

DIRECTIONS

Ted is doing a research report about exercise. First he asked third graders about their exercise habits. He made the graphs below to show what he learned. Use the graphs to answer the questions.

Third Graders' Favorite Ways to Exercise

(bar graph: vertical axis "Number of Third Graders" from 0 to 15; bars — Dance 5, Run 8, Swim 11, Walk 14)

How Often Third Graders Exercise

(pie chart: 52% Often, 16% Very Often, 20% Sometimes, 12% Almost Never)

Foresman 3

1 Swimming is the favorite exercise of how many students?
- ◯ 5
- ◯ 10
- ◯ 11
- ◯ 14

2 Which exercise do the most third graders like best?
- ◯ walking
- ◯ swimming
- ◯ running
- ◯ dancing

3 How many third graders like running best?
- ◯ 2
- ◯ 6
- ◯ 8
- ◯ 12

4 The largest number of third graders exercise —
- ◯ almost never.
- ◯ sometimes.
- ◯ often.
- ◯ very often.

5 What percentage of the third graders exercise "Very often"?
- ◯ 12%
- ◯ 16%
- ◯ 20%
- ◯ 52%

6 The smallest percentage of third graders exercise —
- ◯ sometimes.
- ◯ often.
- ◯ very often.
- ◯ almost never.

GO ON

DIRECTIONS
Ted also looked for information about exercise in a textbook. Read this page from the textbook. Then answer the questions.

Chapter 3: Your Health

Lesson 1: Exercise for Good Health

What Exercise Is
Whenever you use your muscles to do a physical activity, you are getting exercise. Sports such as basketball, swimming, and skating are types of exercise. But so are many hobbies or chores, such as gardening or making a bed.

How Exercise Helps You
Exercise is important for every part of your body. When you are young, you need to exercise to help your bones and muscles form properly. Your balance and strength are better if you exercise. Exercise helps your heart, lungs, and brain do their jobs better. Getting enough exercise helps you sleep well at night. It also helps your body fight off sickness and get better faster when you do get sick.

Exercise and Your Weight
Food is your body's fuel. You burn off this fuel as you go about your daily activities. Exercise burns more fuel than activities such as reading or watching television. The right amount of exercise for the food you eat will keep your weight steady. But if you eat a lot and exercise a little, you will gain weight.

lt Foresman 3

7 What is the title of Chapter 3?
○ Exercise and Your Weight
○ Exercise For Good Health
○ Sleep Well
○ Your Health

8 How many lessons are in this chapter?
○ two
○ three
○ four
○ five

9 In which lesson should Ted look for information about how food can help make people healthy?
○ Lesson 1
○ Lesson 2
○ Lesson 3
○ Lesson 4

10 If Ted wants to learn about why exercise is good for his health, he should read the text under —
○ "How Exercise Helps You."
○ "What Exercise Is."
○ "Exercise and Your Weight."
○ "Practice Good Habits."

STOP

Are We There Yet?

Name _____

Date _____

Scott Foresman
Reading
Grade 3

Editorial Offices
Glenview, Illinois • New York, New York

Sales Offices
Reading, Massachusetts • Duluth, Georgia • Glenview, Illinois
Carrollton, Texas • Menlo Park, California

ISBN 0-673-62426-9

3 4 5 6 7 8 9 10-EBA-06 05 04 03 02 01

READING: Comprehension

DIRECTIONS
Read each passage. Then read each question about the passage. Choose the best answer to each question. Mark the space for your answer.

Animals on the Move

In northern areas, winter is the toughest season for animals. Snow covers the ground like a blanket. Days are cold, and food is scarce. Nobody really likes winter.

A cold winter poses many problems for some animals. Some birds cannot live in the cold. They fly to warmer places for the winter and return in the spring. Other animals, such as frogs and turtles, sleep all winter long.

Many animals, though, stay active throughout the winter. They have different ways of dealing with the problems of cold and snow. Some, like the snowshoe hare, look quite different in winter. During the summer, this rabbit's fur is brown. In the winter, it turns white like the snow. This helps protect the hare from its enemies. It can hide by standing still.

Other animals, such as foxes and bobcats, solve the cold problem by growing thicker fur in winter. The thicker fur helps keep them warm. Because food is scarce, foxes and bobcats often travel far from home looking for food. Like the snowshoe hare, they are mostly active at night.

Animals leave tracks in the snow wherever they go. The tracks are easier to spot in winter than in summer. By studying the tracks, you can tell what animals live nearby even though you might never get to see the animals themselves.

Foresman 3

Animal Tracks

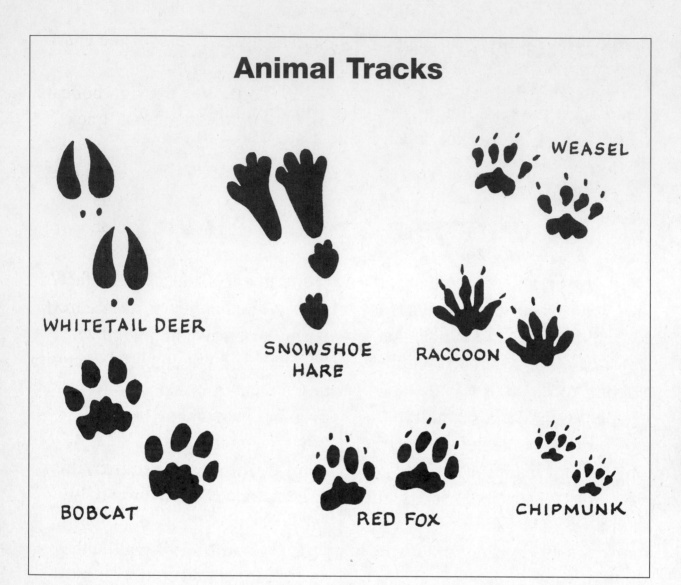

WEASEL

WHITETAIL DEER

SNOWSHOE HARE

RACCOON

BOBCAT

RED FOX

CHIPMUNK

Some animal tracks are very easy to recognize. The whitetail deer, for example, leaves a track that looks like an upside-down heart. The snowshoe hare, with its huge hind feet, leaves large tracks in the snow. A track without claws is a pretty good sign that a cat or bobcat has been around. Unlike the cat's tracks, those made by foxes always show claws.

Winter is an excellent time to study animal tracks. You will enjoy this activity if you try it. The best time of day to look for tracks is early in the morning, before the sun shines on them.

Foresman 3

GO ON

1 What most likely will happen when the sun shines on animal tracks in the snow?
- ○ Animals wake up and walk over the tracks.
- ○ The tracks become easier to see.
- ○ The tracks melt away.
- ○ The tracks become larger.

2 The information in the first four paragraphs of this selection is organized mainly by —
- ○ comparison and contrast.
- ○ problem and solution.
- ○ cause and effect.
- ○ sequence of events.

3 Which is a statement of opinion?
- ○ "Days are cold, and food is scarce."
- ○ "Some birds cannot live in the cold."
- ○ "Animals leave tracks in the snow wherever they go."
- ○ "Winter is an excellent time to study animal tracks."

4 The author includes the chart in this selection to —
- ○ compare hares and bobcats.
- ○ show what animal tracks look like.
- ○ describe how bobcats live.
- ○ explain how animals change in the winter.

5 Which is a statement of fact?
- ○ "Some animal tracks are very easy to recognize."
- ○ "You will enjoy this activity if you try it."
- ○ "Nobody really likes winter."
- ○ "During the summer, this rabbit's fur is brown."

6 In the sentence, "Unlike the cat's tracks, those made by foxes always show claws," the word *Unlike* shows —
- ○ problem and solution.
- ○ time order.
- ○ contrast.
- ○ cause and effect.

Snowflake Bentley

Wilson Bentley was born on a farm in Jericho, Vermont, on February 9, 1865. He loved to learn all he could about the world around him. By the time he was fifteen, Bentley had read an entire encyclopedia.

One day, Wilson Bentley's mother gave him something that would change his life forever. It was a microscope. The microscope made small things look larger and opened up a whole new world for Bentley.

More than anything else in the world, Bentley loved snow. That winter when snow began to fall, he went outside with his microscope. Catching a few snowflakes, he looked at one through the microscope. What he saw amazed him. The ice crystal had a beautiful design. He examined another and another. Each one was different. He wished there were a way to preserve them so other people could see them.

For three winters Bentley tried drawing the snowflakes, but they often melted before he could finish. Then one day he read about a camera with its own microscope. It cost a lot of money. Bentley's parents spent their savings to buy that camera for his seventeenth birthday. It was a great gift.

Bentley spent the next fifty years photographing snowflakes. He became known all over the world as "Snowflake" Bentley.

Bentley dreamed of one day producing a book of his snowflake photographs. It would be his gift to the world, he said. His dream was finally realized in 1931 when *Snow Crystals* was published. The book contained 277 pages of Bentley's photographs. The photos were both interesting and beautiful.

Wilson "Snowflake" Bentley died in 1931, just a few weeks after *Snow Crystals* was published. Bentley's book was a great gift to the world. During his lifetime he photographed 5,381 snowflakes. Today, people who want to learn about snow crystals often begin by reading Bentley's book.

GO ON ➡

t Foresman 3

7 Which is a statement of fact in this selection?

○ "The ice crystal had a beautiful design."

○ "It was a great gift."

○ "The photos were both interesting and beautiful."

○ "During his lifetime he photographed 5,381 snowflakes."

8 How is information in this selection organized?

○ by questions and answers

○ in the order that things happened

○ as problems and solutions

○ as causes and effects

9 Which is a statement of opinion?

○ "The microscope made small things look larger."

○ "Bentley spent the next fifty years photographing snowflakes."

○ "Bentley's book was a great gift to the world."

○ "The book contained 277 pages of Bentley's photographs."

10 A person who wanted to study snow crystals most likely would —

○ go to Jericho, Vermont.

○ read about Bentley's life.

○ read Bentley's book.

○ visit Bentley's home.

11 The author of this selection shows when events took place by —

○ using words such as first and last.

○ giving dates and periods of time.

○ telling the numbers of pages and photographs.

○ including a time line.

12 The author's main purpose in this selection is to —

○ explain what a microscope does.

○ tell how to photograph snowflakes.

○ persuade people to read Bentley's book.

○ give information about Wilson Bentley.

Foresman 3

GO ON

What Little White Bird Saw

The sun had not yet risen when Little White Bird left the Nez Percé camp in Oregon. It was a summer day in 1877. Little White Bird knew that the U.S. Army wanted his people to leave their land, and he needed to decide what to do. He walked all day under the hot sun, letting his feet <u>lead</u> him where they would. Just as the sun was starting to set, Little White Bird realized he couldn't walk any farther. He was too tired.

Little White Bird built a small fire, cooked and ate a young <u>hare</u>, and sat down to wait. He remembered Chief Joseph's words from the day before. "Great Spirit Chief comes when you are ready to listen." Little White Bird yawned. He was ready, but he was so tired. The smoke rising from his fire looked like shadowy men. Soon Little White Bird was sound asleep.

Great Spirit Chief came to Little White Bird as an eagle. "Your people will one day be forced to move from the Wallowa Valley," he said.

"But why?" asked Little White Bird.

"The White Man is greedy," said Great Spirit Chief. "He plans to move your people to a reservation in Idaho so he can have your land."

"We won't go!" cried Little White Bird. "This is our land. We have a treaty that says so."

"That may be," said Great Spirit Chief, "but the White Man will not keep his promise."

"What can I do?" asked Little White Bird.

"One day you shall be Chief White Bird. You'll do whatever you believe is best for your people."

Just then, Little White Bird woke up. He knew he would become a chief someday, and he knew that he did not want his people to leave Oregon. He wasted no time getting back to the camp. He had something very important that he needed to do.

Foresman 3

GO ON →

13 What will Little White Bird most likely do when he gets back to camp?

○ He will tell Chief Joseph what he has learned.

○ He will demand that he be made chief right away.

○ He will tear up the treaty between the Nez Percé and the United States.

○ He will tell his people that they should move to Idaho.

14 In this passage, the word <u>lead</u> means —

○ to spend time.

○ the part of a pencil used for writing.

○ to show the way.

○ a place in front.

15 In this passage, the word <u>hare</u> means —

○ something you can hear.

○ something that grows on people's heads.

○ a large rabbit.

○ nearby.

16 The author's main purpose in this passage is to —

○ explain how treaties are made.

○ describe where the Nez Percé lived.

○ give information about the Nez Percé.

○ tell a story about a young man.

17 What kind of selection is this?

○ play

○ fable

○ historical fiction

○ biography

18 Which sentence contains a simile?

○ "The smoke rising from his fire looked like shadowy men."

○ "He walked all day under the hot sun."

○ "Little White Bird built a small fire."

○ "Just then, Little White Bird woke up."

GO ON ➤

tt Foresman 3

Prepared for Takeoff!

Tori James had never been away from home for more than a few days. But now she was a bird getting ready to fly. A <u>week</u> or two at a summer camp would be nice, she thought. The only question was, what kind of camp? Tori was not very good at sports or music, so those kinds of camps were out. There's got to be some kind of camp out there for kids like me, thought Tori, but what?

She picked up her copy of *Kids Today* and began thumbing through it. On the last page she saw something that made her smile. It was an ad for a space camp. She decided to <u>tear</u> out the ad.

"That's it!" cried Tori. "That's the camp for me." She picked up the phone and dialed the number on the ad. The line was busy. She tried several more times that afternoon, but the line was always busy.

At dinner that night, Tori told her family all about the space camp she wanted to attend. Mom asked how much it would cost. "I don't know yet," said Tori, "but I'll find out pretty soon."

Take Off for Fun and Adventure!

Do you ever wonder what it would be like to live and work in space? Well, here's your chance to find out. At the Supernova Space Camp for Kids, you will

- wear a space suit
- sleep on a spaceship
- eat space food
- build your own rocket
- train for a special mission
- and have lots of fun!

Call now for more information!
1-800-555-1378

tt Foresman 3

19 After dinner, Tori most likely will —

○ offer to wash the dishes.
○ make another phone call.
○ go outside and play.
○ do her homework.

20 What kind of selection is this?

○ realistic fiction
○ historical fiction
○ biography
○ fable

21 In this selection, the word <u>tear</u> means —

○ a drop falling from the eye.
○ rip or pull apart.
○ get sleepy.
○ a wheel on a car.

22 The main purpose of the ad in this selection is to —

○ describe life on a spaceship.
○ persuade readers to call for information.
○ give information about space travel.
○ explain how to live in space.

23 Which sentence contains a metaphor?

○ "But now she was a bird getting ready to fly."
○ "Tori was not very good at sports or music."
○ "On the last page she saw something that made her smile."
○ "It was an ad for a space camp."

24 In this selection, the word <u>week</u> means —

○ get up from sleeping.
○ seven days.
○ not strong.
○ waves stirred up by a boat.

STOP

READING: Phonics

DIRECTIONS

Read the word. Find the word that has the same sound as the underlined letter or letters. Mark the space for your answer.

25 li<u>k</u>e
- ○ race
- ○ knee
- ○ fill
- ○ ache

26 <u>wh</u>o
- ○ when
- ○ wide
- ○ home
- ○ phone

27 <u>wh</u>at
- ○ while
- ○ draw
- ○ hold
- ○ slow

28 <u>c</u>oat
- ○ which
- ○ decide
- ○ knit
- ○ rake

29 pa<u>ck</u>
- ○ city
- ○ know
- ○ came
- ○ chin

30 <u>wh</u>ole
- ○ hand
- ○ well
- ○ where
- ○ week

31 <u>h</u>ug
- ○ push
- ○ whose
- ○ path
- ○ white

32 tri<u>ck</u>
- ○ witch
- ○ cider
- ○ lake
- ○ much

tt Foresman 3

DIRECTIONS

Choose the prefix that can be added to the base word to form a new word with the meaning "not." Mark the space for your answer.

33 agree
- ○ im-
- ○ dis-
- ○ pre-
- ○ non-

34 patient
- ○ re-
- ○ sub-
- ○ un-
- ○ im-

35 sense
- ○ non-
- ○ im-
- ○ dis-
- ○ un-

36 appear
- ○ un-
- ○ dis-
- ○ non-
- ○ im-

DIRECTIONS

Read each sentence. Choose the correct form of the word that fits in the blank. Mark the space for your answer.

37 I _____ to call you last night.
- ◯ tryed
- ◯ tried
- ◯ try
- ◯ trying

38 This train will be _____ at the next station.
- ◯ stoped
- ◯ stop
- ◯ stoping
- ◯ stopping

39 Which of these three books is the _____ to read?
- ◯ easyer
- ◯ easyest
- ◯ easiest
- ◯ easy

40 Today is _____ than yesterday.
- ◯ hotter
- ◯ hoter
- ◯ hottest
- ◯ hotest

GO ON

t Foresman 3

41 Ms. Brant is the _____ person I know.

- ○ nicer
- ○ nice
- ○ niceest
- ○ nicest

42 Carlos has many baseball _____.

- ○ card
- ○ cards
- ○ card's
- ○ cardes

43 The boys threw _____ in the pond.

- ○ stone
- ○ stones
- ○ stone's
- ○ stonees

44 The _____ stole our money.

- ○ thiefs
- ○ thief's
- ○ thiefes
- ○ thieves

45 Ariel caught two _____.

- ○ mouse
- ○ mouses
- ○ mice
- ○ mices

STOP

t Foresman 3

WRITING/GRAMMAR

DIRECTIONS

Read each passage. Choose the word that best fits in each numbered blank. Mark the space for your answer.

Andrea and _____ found an old bottle on the beach. There
      (1)

was a message inside. _____ took the message out. It was a note
      (2)

from a boy in Sweden, and it gave _____ name and address.
      (3)

That bottle had traveled from Sweden all the way to Maine! Can

you believe it?

---

1 ○ me
   ○ i
   ○ us
   ○ I

2 ○ We
   ○ Us
   ○ Them
   ○ Her

3 ○ him
   ○ his
   ○ ours
   ○ hers

GO ON ➤

Foresman 3

Mario's family decided to go camping. They were hoping to stay

_____ the ocean. They got to the campground at five, _____ they
(4)   (5)
were too late. All the best camping spots were already taken.

4 ○ near
   ○ in
   ○ for
   ○ below

5 ○ or
   ○ and
   ○ because
   ○ but

STOP

WRITING

Brianna has done some research on the life of Beryl Markham, a famous pilot and author. Use these notes to write a report about Beryl Markham. Choose the information you want to use and organize it for your report.

Notes on Beryl Clutterback Markham

- Born October 26, 1902
- Died August 2, 1986
- Moved to Kenya, a country in eastern Africa, when she was three
- 1936: first person to fly alone across the Atlantic Ocean (from London, England, to Nova Scotia, Canada)
- Born in Leicester, England
- Pilot and horse trainer
- Successful horse trainer in Kenya from 1958 to 1972
- Learned to speak several African languages
- Wrote a book, *West With the Night*
- Died in Kenya at age 84
- Married Mansfield Markham in 1927
- *West With the Night* published in 1942

Prewriting Notes

GO ON

tt Foresman 3

STUDY SKILLS

DIRECTIONS

Alana is writing a report on Native American tribes in the United States. She found this map on a CD-ROM atlas. Use the map to answer the questions.

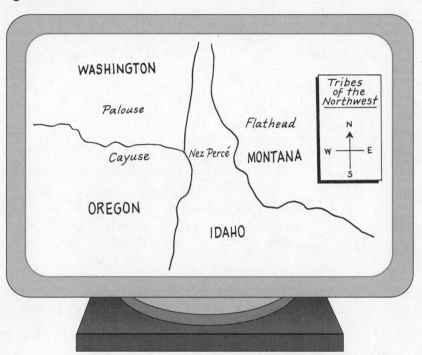

1 Which tribe lived in the center of Washington?
   ○ Flathead
   ○ Nez Percé
   ○ Palouse
   ○ Cayuse

2 Which tribe lived in Montana?
   ○ Flathead
   ○ Nez Percé
   ○ Palouse
   ○ Cayuse

3 If Alana wants to find a map of the Great Lakes in this atlas, she should —
   ○ click on "Washington."
   ○ type "Great" on the screen.
   ○ click on "Nez Percé."
   ○ go to the index or table of contents.

Foresman 3

GO ON

Alana found this chart of information about where Native American tribes lived. Use the chart to answer the questions.

Tribes of the Southwest	
Tribe	**Where They Lived**
Apache	New Mexico and Arizona
Comanche	Texas
Hopi	Arizona
Kiowa	Oklahoma
Navajo	Arizona
Zuni	New Mexico

4 Where did the Comanches live?
- ○ Arizona
- ○ Oklahoma
- ○ New Mexico
- ○ Texas

5 Which two tribes both lived in New Mexico?
- ○ Zuni and Apache
- ○ Navajo and Hopi
- ○ Comanche and Zuni
- ○ Kiowa and Navajo

6 Which tribe lived in what are now two different states?
- ○ Navajo
- ○ Zuni
- ○ Apache
- ○ Comanche

7 Where did the Kiowa live?
- ○ Texas
- ○ Arizona
- ○ Oklahoma
- ○ New Mexico

GO ON

Alana found this time line in a book. Use the time line below to answer the questions.

Nez Percé acquire horses	Lewis and Clark arrive	Young Joseph becomes chief War with U.S.	Chief Joseph dies	2,000 Nez Percé now living on reservation in Idaho
early 1700s	1805	1877	1904	1999

8 When did Joseph become chief of the Nez Percé?
- ◯ early 1700s
- ◯ 1805
- ◯ 1877
- ◯ 1876

9 What happened in 1904?
- ◯ Chief Joseph died.
- ◯ The Nez Percé acquired horses.
- ◯ Lewis and Clark arrived.
- ◯ The Nez Percé went to war with the U.S.

10 How many Nez Percé are now living in Idaho?
- ◯ 1,805
- ◯ 1,877
- ◯ 1,904
- ◯ 2,000

STOP

t Foresman 3

Imagination.kids

Name _____

Date _____

Scott Foresman
Reading
Grade 3

Editorial Offices
Glenview, Illinois • New York, New York

Sales Offices
Reading, Massachusetts • Duluth, Georgia • Glenview, Illinois
Carrollton, Texas • Menlo Park, California

ISBN 0-673-62427-7

3 4 5 6 7 8 9 10-EBA-06 05 04 03 02 01

READING: Comprehension

DIRECTIONS

Read each passage. Then read each question about the passage. Choose the best answer to each question. Mark the space for your answer.

Shuttle to Freedom

Have you ever wondered what it would be like to live in space? It's possible that years from now some people may actually be living and working on a space station. Who knows, you might even be one of them.

Back in 1984, the people at NASA (the National Aeronautics and Space Administration) started making plans to build a space station called *Freedom*. This space station, built in space, would stay in space forever. People would live and work there. They would use a space shuttle to travel back and forth between Earth and *Freedom*. A space shuttle is a kind of spaceship. It carries people into

space and then flies back to Earth, where it can <u>land</u> on a runway the same way a jet plane does.

Even though a model of *Freedom* has been built, the space station itself has not yet been built in space. Space projects cost a lot of money. For now anyway, a space station is still only a dream for the future.

Space shuttles, however, have already been built and are being used. The shuttle is made up of three main parts. The part that carries the people is called the orbiter. This part can be used over and over again. The other two parts of the shuttle are a red fuel tank and two rockets.

Foresman 3

GO ON ➡

Unit 6 Skills Test **1**

Space Shuttle

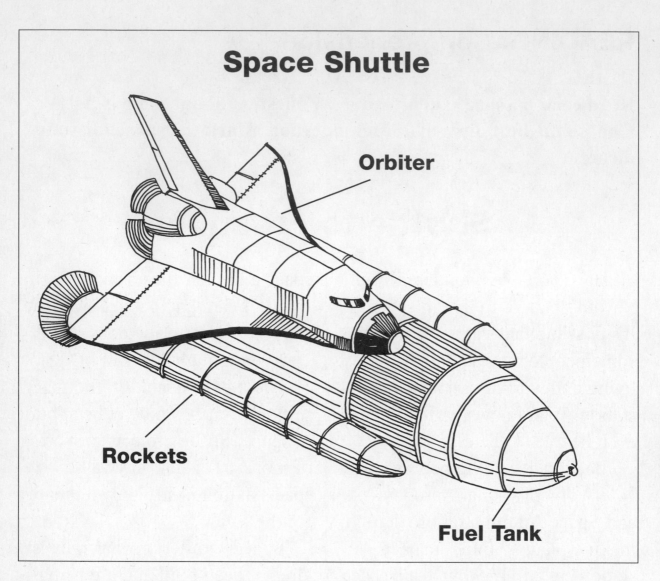

Orbiter

Rockets

Fuel Tank

The rockets help blast the shuttle into space. Two minutes after takeoff, the rockets drop off. They fall into the Atlantic Ocean. A ship comes by later and picks them up. The rockets, too, can be used again.

After the shuttle enters space, the fuel tank comes off. It burns up in the air as it falls back to Earth. This is the only part of the shuttle that cannot be reused.

Today, space shuttles carry people into space and back. The people live and work inside the shuttle. They return to Earth after a few days. If and when a space station is finally built, space shuttles will be used to take people back and forth.

Foresman 3

GO ON

1 Which is a generalization?
- ○ "Two minutes after takeoff, the rockets drop off."
- ○ "The shuttle is made up of three main parts."
- ○ "Space projects cost a lot of money."
- ○ "The rockets help blast the shuttle into space."

2 Which is most likely to happen years from now?
- ○ Everyone will move to space stations.
- ○ A space station will be built in space.
- ○ NASA will stop going into space.
- ○ Space travel will no longer cost money.

3 From what this selection says, it is most likely true that —
- ○ space shuttles are used a lot by NASA.
- ○ everyone wants to go into space.
- ○ space shuttles are too noisy.
- ○ everyone likes to travel.

4 Using parts of the shuttle over again is a good idea because it helps NASA to —
- ○ build bigger shuttles.
- ○ save money.
- ○ send more people into space.
- ○ make plans for a space station.

5 In this selection, the word land means —
- ○ the solid part of Earth's surface.
- ○ to go on shore from a ship or boat.
- ○ a country or particular place.
- ○ to come down from the air; come to rest.

GO ON

tt Foresman 3

Why Coyotes Are Not Blue

At one time, bluebirds and coyotes lived near a lake where the water was a bright, bright blue. Back then, bluebirds were a very ugly color. One day a bluebird decided to change his color, so he jumped right into that bright blue water.

Coyote happened to be strolling by just then. What was Bluebird up to, he wondered. Curious, he crept closer and hid behind a bush to watch. Bluebird splashed around a bit before he began to sing:

Soaking in this lake so blue
Under a blue sky, as I do,
When I come out, I'll be all
*   blue too.*

Then Bluebird hopped out of the water and shook himself dry. He was still the same ugly color. For four mornings in a row, Bluebird came to bathe in the lake. Each time he sang the same song. On the fourth morning, when Bluebird came out of the water, he was missing all his feathers. Coyote gasped. Bluebird was even uglier than before.

On the fifth morning, when Bluebird came out of the water, he had bright blue feathers. Coyote couldn't believe it! He jumped out of the bushes. "How can this be?" he asked. "You were ugly before, but now you are beautiful. I want to be blue just like you."

Bluebird told Coyote what to do and taught him the song. Coyote did as he was told. When he came out of the lake, he was just as blue as Bluebird. This made Coyote feel very proud.

Coyote pranced home glancing from side to side and all around to see if anyone noticed how beautiful and blue he was. He forgot to watch where he was going and ran into a stump so hard it knocked him down into the dirt. When Coyote got up, he wasn't blue anymore. He was covered with dust all over. That's why, to this day, all coyotes are the color of dirt.

it Foresman 3

GO ON

6 What happened in the beginning of this story?

○ Bluebird changed color.
○ Coyote sang a song.
○ Bluebird jumped into a lake.
○ Coyote ran into a stump.

7 Where does this story take place?

○ in a forest
○ in a zoo
○ in a city park
○ at a lake

8 When does this story take place?

○ in the future
○ long ago
○ in the present
○ a year ago

9 What happened at the end of this story?

○ Coyote fell in the dirt.
○ Bluebird sang a song.
○ Coyote asked Bluebird for help.
○ Bluebird lost his feathers.

10 In this passage, the word <u>watch</u> means —

○ a device for telling time.
○ to look; pay attention to.
○ a person who guards or protects.
○ to keep guard.

GO ON ▶

Something to Share

Keisha raced home from school and ran upstairs to Nana's room. She couldn't wait to tell Nana the good news. Her drawing had won second place in the student art show. Keisha came to a halt just outside Nana's bedroom. She sighed when she saw Nana asleep in her chair, a sad crooked smile on her face. How could she have forgotten?

Keisha walked in and knelt beside Nana's chair. She took Nana's limp hand into hers. When she looked up, she found Nana's eyes on her. They had a faraway look in them. Mama had said it would probably take a long time for Nana to recover from her <u>stroke</u>. Keisha sighed. She missed the old Nana, the one who loved to read books and to draw.

"I have good news, Nana," said Keisha, gently squeezing Nana's hand. "I won second place in the art show." She lay her head on Nana's lap. "I miss you so much," she said softly. "I wish we could still do things together." Keisha felt Nana's fingers move inside her hand. She looked up in surprise. Nana's eyes seemed brighter. Just then Keisha had an idea. She suddenly knew what she needed to do.

Keisha ran downstairs and returned a few minutes later, her arms loaded with books and assorted art supplies. She dumped everything on the floor by Nana's chair. Then she picked up a bright red marker and a pad of paper. She placed the marker in Nana's hand and wrapped her own hand around both. Gently she guided Nana's hand, drawing a pretty red tulip on the pad.

A few tulips later, Nana was obviously tiring. Keisha and her mom helped Nana to her bed. Keisha chose one of her favorite books and climbed into bed beside Nana. In a soft voice, she began to read until Nana fell asleep. Keisha smiled. It wasn't quite the same as it used to be, but it was a good start.

GO ON

tt Foresman 3

11 Where does this story take place?
- ◯ at a school
- ◯ in a bedroom
- ◯ in a hospital
- ◯ in a park

12 What does Keisha miss most?
- ◯ spending time with her friends
- ◯ taking naps with Nana
- ◯ reading and drawing with Nana
- ◯ listening to Nana's stories

13 What happens in the middle of this story?
- ◯ Keisha tells Nana some news.
- ◯ Nana draws a tulip by herself.
- ◯ Keisha reads a book.
- ◯ Nana goes to bed.

14 From what this story says, it is most likely true that —
- ◯ everyone loves art.
- ◯ many old people can't do all the things they used to do.
- ◯ older people are always sad.
- ◯ most people fall asleep when they read or listen to stories.

15 In this passage, the word <u>stroke</u> means —
- ◯ a piece of luck.
- ◯ a movement made with a pen.
- ◯ a movement made by a swimmer.
- ◯ a sudden attack of illness.

GO ON

Lost in . . . the Mail?

"I know it's in here somewhere," said Tomás, still looking for the paper from school. He pulled a half-eaten apple out of his backpack. "Yuck!" he said, throwing the apple into the garbage. He continued to search. "Here it is," he said at last. He held up a crumpled piece of paper. "Our class is going to visit the post office tomorrow," he said. "You need to sign this to say I can go." Tomás gave the paper to his mom.

"I didn't know you had a pen pal in Costa Rica," said Tomás's mom as she signed the form.

"I almost forgot," Tomás gasped. "I need to find Geraldo's letter to get his address," he said, reaching for his backpack. "I know it's in here somewhere."

Mrs. Sanchez chuckled. "Letters always get lost in the mail," she said, "but never in a backpack."

"Aha!" cried Tomás, pulling out a ragged envelope. "I found it." He sat down at the kitchen table to write a letter to his pen pal. "Have you seen my pen?" he asked. Mrs. Sanchez rolled her eyes. "Never mind," said Tomás, reaching for his backpack. "I know it's in here somewhere."

Dear Parent(s),

    Ms. Gomez's third-grade class will be visiting the post office on Tuesday, March 22. Students will mail letters to pen pals in Costa Rica and learn how the mail gets from here to there. To give your child permission for this trip, please sign below.

_____ can go to the post office with Ms. Gomez's third-grade class.

                Signed _____

Foresman 3

GO ON ➤

16 Where does this story take place?
- ○ at Tomás's school
- ○ at Tomás's house
- ○ at the library
- ○ at the post office

17 Which sentence is a generalization?
- ○ "He continued to search."
- ○ "Letters always get lost in the mail."
- ○ "He sat down at the kitchen table."
- ○ "Mrs. Sanchez rolled her eyes."

18 What is Tomás's biggest problem?
- ○ He has a pen pal.
- ○ He has to go to the post office.
- ○ He keeps losing things.
- ○ He found an old apple in his backpack.

19 What happens at the beginning of this story?
- ○ Tomás sits down to write a letter.
- ○ Tomás eats an apple.
- ○ Tomás goes to the post office.
- ○ Tomás finds the letter from Ms. Gomez and gives it to his mom.

20 In this passage, the word <u>pen</u> means —
- ○ a small closed yard for animals.
- ○ to shut in.
- ○ a tool used for writing.
- ○ to write.

STOP

Foresman 3

READING: Phonics

DIRECTIONS

Read the word. Find the word that has the same sound as the underlined letter or letters. Mark the space for your answer.

21 ca<u>u</u>se
- ○ drum
- ○ drape
- ○ dream
- ○ draw

22 gr<u>ew</u>
- ○ saw
- ○ suit
- ○ seat
- ○ slow

23 l<u>aw</u>
- ○ stair
- ○ stall
- ○ stay
- ○ still

24 j<u>ui</u>ce
- ○ flip
- ○ flat
- ○ flew
- ○ fly

25 t<u>u</u>be
- ○ chew
- ○ chat
- ○ chop
- ○ chain

26 s<u>au</u>ce
- ○ lean
- ○ loan
- ○ lone
- ○ lawn

27 t<u>al</u>k
- ○ caught
- ○ cat
- ○ coat
- ○ cut

28 st<u>ew</u>
- ○ blow
- ○ build
- ○ bruise
- ○ bowl

GO ON ▶

Foresman 3

DIRECTIONS
Find the base word of each underlined word. Mark the space for your answer.

29 thoughtful
- ◯ thou
- ◯ ought
- ◯ thought
- ◯ ful

30 disappear
- ◯ pear
- ◯ appear
- ◯ dis
- ◯ ear

31 replace
- ◯ re
- ◯ rep
- ◯ place
- ◯ lace

32 untruthfully
- ◯ un
- ◯ truth
- ◯ ful
- ◯ fully

Find the prefix in each underlined word.

33 distasteful
- ◯ taste
- ◯ ful
- ◯ distaste
- ◯ dis

34 unkindly
- ◯ un
- ◯ kind
- ◯ kindly
- ◯ ly

Find the suffix in each underlined word.

35 priceless
- ◯ price
- ◯ rice
- ◯ less
- ◯ ess

36 unreadable
- ◯ un
- ◯ read
- ◯ unread
- ◯ able

GO ON

DIRECTIONS
Choose the word that is divided into syllables correctly. Mark the space for your answer.

37 ◯ sudd • enly
◯ ope • ned
◯ un • der • stand
◯ star • ting

38 ◯ que • stion
◯ onl • y
◯ cryi • ng
◯ hope • less

39 ◯ some • thing
◯ no • body
◯ ca • rpool
◯ any • whe • re

40 ◯ answe • r
◯ slee • ping
◯ ci • rcle
◯ um • brel • la

STOP

t Foresman 3

WRITING/GRAMMAR

DIRECTIONS

Read each passage. Some parts are underlined. The underlined parts may have mistakes in the way they are written or in the use of punctuation. Mark the space beside the best way to write each underlined part. If the underlined part needs no change, mark the choice "No mistake."

Nigel and his cousin visited the Space and Rocket Center.

They met an astronaut, and she gave them a tour. The boys
(1)
learned a lot about rockets and space shuttles. Now Nigel and
(2)
his cousin wants to be astronauts.

---

1 ○ They met an astronaut. And she gave them a tour.
  ○ They met an astronaut and gave them a tour.
  ○ They met an astronaut she gave them a tour.
  ○ No mistake

2 ○ Now Nigel and his cousin want to be astronauts.
  ○ Now Nigel and his cousin wanting to be astronauts.
  ○ Now Nigel and his cousin is wanting to be astronauts.
  ○ No mistake

Foresman 3

GO ON

January, 12, 2000
_____
(3)

Dear Nikki,

   I just bought some pearls, beads, and string. We can make
  (4)

necklaces next weekend when you come to visit. Also, Ashley is

having a sleepover on Saturday night. She said, Tell Nikki to bring
                   (5)

a sleeping bag. If you don't have one, I have an extra one you can

use.

          Your friend,
          Jenny

---

3 ○ January 12 2000,
   ○ January, 12 2000
   ○ January 12, 2000
   ○ No mistake

4 ○ I just bought some pearls, beads, and, string.
   ○ I just bought some pearls beads, and string.
   ○ I just bought some pearls beads and string.
   ○ No mistake

5 ○ She said, "Tell Nikki to bring a sleeping bag."
   ○ "She said, Tell Nikki to bring a sleeping bag."
   ○ She said, "Tell Nikki to bring a sleeping bag".
   ○ No mistake

STOP

Foresman 3

WRITING

Some parents give their children an allowance each week. An allowance is an amount of money paid for doing jobs around the house. Write a persuasive letter to a parent telling him or her why you think you should get an allowance. If you already get an allowance, tell why you think your allowance should be higher. Give reasons in your letter. Use correct form for a friendly letter.

Prewriting Notes

GO ON

tt Foresman 3

_____

_____

_____

_____

_____

_____

_____

_____

_____

tt Foresman 3

STOP

STUDY SKILLS

DIRECTIONS

Raoul and his friends are looking for something to do over the weekend. Raoul saw this poster. Use the poster to answer the questions.

ARTS & CRAFTS SALE!

WHERE: Parkhurst Elementary School gym

WHEN: Saturday, October 14
9:30 A.M. – 5:00 P.M.
and
Sunday, October 15
10:00 A.M. – 1:00 P.M.

Jewelry • Candles • Pottery • Dried Flowers

Free cookies for students and their parents!

---

1 Where is the Arts & Crafts Sale being held?
- ○ at someone's house
- ○ at a store in the mall
- ○ in a school gym
- ○ in a church basement

2 At what time does the sale end on Saturday?
- ○ 9:30 A.M.
- ○ 10:00 A.M.
- ○ 1:00 P.M.
- ○ 5:00 P.M.

GO ON ▶

tt Foresman 3

3 At what time does the sale start on Sunday?
- ○ 9:30 A.M.
- ○ 10:00 A.M.
- ○ 1:00 P.M.
- ○ 5:00 P.M.

4 Which of these does not cost anything?
- ○ cookies
- ○ candles
- ○ jewelry
- ○ dried flowers

5 This poster was written to —
- ○ describe how arts and crafts are made.
- ○ list the prices of arts and crafts.
- ○ persuade people to go to the sale.
- ○ give directions to the school.

STOP

Foresman 3

DIRECTIONS

Raoul looks in the newspaper for other things to do. Use these parts of a newspaper to answer the questions.

Yard Sale Neighborhood sale of toys, furniture, games, and much more. Saturday, 9 to 5. Beacon Street.

Student Wins Spelling Bee
by Brent Campbell
Joan Washington, a third grader at Parkhurst Elementary School, won first prize in the citywide spelling bee. The last word she had to spell to win was *gnome*.

Green-Up Day
The annual Green-Up Day will be held Saturday. We think this is a great event. We all want our town to be clean and beautiful. To keep it that way, everyone has to help. We urge everyone to get out there and help "green up" our city.

Soccer Team Wins!
by Colin Jones
In an exciting game, the Red Dogs beat the Mostown Raiders yesterday 2 to 1. With that win, the Red Dogs will go on to the final game on Saturday. The game will begin at 1:00 P.M. at the Parkhurst field.

GO ON

t Foresman 3

6 "Student Wins Spelling Bee" is an example of —

○ an editorial.

○ a news story.

○ an advertisement.

○ a sports article.

7 Which part is a classified ad?

○ "Yard Sale"

○ "Green-Up Day"

○ "Student Wins Spelling Bee"

○ "Soccer Team Wins"

8 "Green-Up Day" is an example of —

○ an editorial.

○ a news story.

○ an advertisement.

○ a sports article.

9 "Soccer Team Wins!" would be in what part of the newspaper?

○ advertisements

○ news

○ letters to the editor

○ sports

10 Which of these is a headline?

○ "Yard Sale"

○ by Brent Campbell

○ "Student Wins Spelling Bee"

○ by Colin Jones

STOP

tt Foresman 3

End-of-Year Skills Test

Name _____

Date _____

Scott Foresman
Reading
Grade 3

Editorial Offices
Glenview, Illinois • New York, New York

Sales Offices
Reading, Massachusetts • Duluth, Georgia • Glenview, Illinois
Carrollton, Texas • Menlo Park, California

ISBN 0-673-62448-X

3 4 5 6 7 8 9 10-EBA-06 05 04 03 02 01

READING: Comprehension

DIRECTIONS
Read each passage. Then read the questions that follow. Choose the best answer to each question. Mark the space beside your answer.

Hawk Eye

The old man was tired. He had been walking across the desert all day. Both he and his horse were moving as slowly as snails. The man longed for a cold drink and some sleep.

He thought about what lay ahead. He knew that he would come to the waterfall before long. Its cool, clear water was not far away now. He would take a big drink and then a nice cool bath.

He trudged on slowly across the sand and the dusty hills. Then he saw it at last! The beautiful waterfall was still there, bubbling down through the rocks. He tied up his horse and walked over to the waterfall.

The old man reached out with his tin cup, eager for a drink. But suddenly a hawk in the sky dove toward the man. The bird shot down and knocked the cup from his hand. Then it flew back up to the clouds.

"Stupid bird," the man said. He picked up his cup and reached for the water again.

A second time, the hawk dove and knocked down the cup. The man was furious. "Go away!" he shouted to the hawk.

A third time, the old man stretched toward the water. And a third time, the hawk knocked the cup from his hand.

"That does it!" the man shouted. He threw a rock and hit the bird between the wings. The hawk flew away.

To make sure he was not bothered again, the man climbed up to the pool above. Some rocks there would block the hawk's path if it came back. The old man reached forward to dip his cup into the deep, clear pool.

That's when he saw the snake. It was dead, floating on the surface of the water. The old man realized at once that its poison had tainted the water. He had not seen the snake from below—but the hawk could see it. The hawk was not being a pest. It had saved the old man's life.

The old man found water from a different stream that night. As he rested, he thought long and hard about the hawk. He decided that in the future he would think more carefully and try not to lose his temper.

GO ON ➤

t Foresman 3

1 From this story you can tell that the old man —
- ○ expected to find the snake in the water.
- ○ was not used to walking in the desert.
- ○ had been bothered by the hawk before.
- ○ had been to the waterfall before.

2 What will the old man most likely do the next time a bird or an animal bothers him?
- ○ He will throw a rock at it.
- ○ He will run away from it.
- ○ He will think about why it is bothering him.
- ○ He will ignore the bird or animal.

3 In this story, the word <u>tainted</u> means —
- ○ caused to flow.
- ○ spoiled; made unclean.
- ○ changed the color of.
- ○ filled; made deeper.

4 Which sentence from the story contains a simile?
- ○ "The old man was tired."
- ○ "He had been walking across the desert all day."
- ○ "Both he and his horse were moving as slowly as snails."
- ○ "The man longed for a cold drink and some sleep."

5 Where does this story take place?
- ○ in a desert
- ○ beside a lake
- ○ in a forest
- ○ on a mountaintop

Foresman 3

Lake Superior

Which is the biggest lake in the world? If you ask an expert this question, you may not get a straight answer. The largest lake in the world is the Caspian Sea in Asia. But it is a saltwater lake, so it is called a "sea." The largest freshwater lake in the world is Lake Superior. It is one of the five Great Lakes. Four of the Great Lakes lie between the United States and Canada. Only Lake Michigan is entirely in the United States.

Lake Superior covers 31,700 square miles. It has the greatest area of any freshwater lake, but it is not the longest or the deepest.

The longest lake in the world is Lake Tanganyika in Africa. It stretches 420 miles, which is seventy miles longer than Superior. Lake Baikal in Russia is the deepest lake. At its deepest point, the bottom of Lake Baikal lies more than a mile below the surface.

Even Superior's claim to the greatest size may not be true. Lake Michigan and Lake Huron are connected by the Mackinac Strait. These two lakes share water back and forth through the strait, so they could be considered one lake. That one lake would be larger than Lake Superior.

World's Largest Freshwater Lakes		
Lake	Area (sq mi)	Location
Superior	31,700	North America
Victoria	26,828	Africa
Huron	23,000	North America
Michigan	22,300	North America
Tanganyika	12,700	Africa
Baikal	12,162	Asia

6 What is the main idea of this passage?

○ The world has many large lakes.

○ Other lakes may be deeper or longer, but Lake Superior has the greatest area of any freshwater lake.

○ Lake Superior lies between the United States and Canada.

○ Lake Tanganyika in Africa is the longest lake in the world.

7 How is Lake Michigan different from Lake Superior?

○ It is entirely in the United States.

○ It is larger.

○ It has salt water.

○ It is deeper.

8 Most of the information in this passage is presented by —

○ causes and effects.

○ steps in a process.

○ time order.

○ comparison and contrast.

9 From the chart, you can tell that Lake Victoria is in —

○ Asia.

○ Africa.

○ the United States.

○ Canada.

10 The Caspian Sea is called a "sca" because it is —

○ located in Asia.

○ larger than Lake Superior.

○ filled with salt water.

○ deeper than other lakes.

Foresman 3

August 18

Dear Maria,

I just spent all weekend sitting on my porch reading *The Sand and the Sun.* It's a great book. I think you should read it soon. You'll love it.

The book is about a family that goes camping in the foothills of the Sangre de Cristo Mountains in New Mexico. They drive for a long time, and they get on each other's nerves. The car's air conditioning shuts down, so they drive across the desert with their windows open. The kids in the back seat get *covered* with sand!

The first part of the book is funny. The parents and the kids find all sorts of ways to pick fights. They come up with some pretty surprising things to say about each other. But then the story gets <u>serious</u>. When they get close to the mountains, their car breaks down. They have to set up their camp in the desert. They are stuck for two weeks before someone else drives down that road, so they are on their own. The rest of the book is about how they learn to survive—but also how they learn to get along and appreciate each other. Each person in the family turns out to be quite special, but none of them could see that at the beginning.

Anyway, I have to go now. I just thought you might like to hear about this book. If you get a chance, check it out of the library and read it. But be prepared to spend your weekend sitting on your porch!

Sincerely,
Angela

Foresman 3

11 What happened first to the family in the book?
  ○ Their car breaks down.
  ○ They get stuck in the desert.
  ○ They set up camp.
  ○ The car's air conditioning shuts down.

12 Which sentence states an opinion?
  ○ "The kids in the back seat get *covered* with sand!"
  ○ "It's a great book."
  ○ "When they get close to the mountains, their car breaks down."
  ○ "They have to set up their camp in the desert."

13 Which word means the opposite of <u>serious</u> in this passage?
  ○ fast
  ○ exciting
  ○ sad
  ○ funny

14 Which phrase from the letter is an idiom?
  ○ "camping in the foothills"
  ○ "with their windows open"
  ○ "get on each other's nerves"
  ○ "sitting on your porch"

15 Angela wrote this letter to —
  ○ persuade Maria to read *The Sand and the Sun.*
  ○ describe her summer vacation.
  ○ entertain Maria with a funny story.
  ○ inform Maria about the Sangre de Cristo Mountains.

GO ON

How to Play Oware

The African pit-and-pebble game of Oware has many names in many languages. Today it is played throughout the world. It is easy to learn, but winning takes a lot of skill and careful thinking.

The game is played on a board that has twelve pits carved in two rows of six each. To start, about three dozen small stones are divided evenly among the pits. The first player chooses a pit and scoops out the stones in it. Then, moving around the board to the right, the player drops one stone in each pit. When the last stone has been dropped, the player takes all the stones in that last pit and sets them to one side. It is then the next player's turn to choose a pit and move the stones. The game ends when all the stones have been taken.

The goal is to collect the greatest number of stones. On each turn, players try to choose the best pit to scoop out. During the game, some pits will have more stones than others. The players try to figure out the starting place that will let them end on the pit with the most stones. At times, none of the pits has the right number of stones to let a player end at a good point. The best players plan their moves several turns ahead of time.

Many games can be boring, but Oware is simple, portable, and fun to play. If you do not have a board with pits, you can play the game on cardboard or dirt. Draw squares or circles for pits.

Oware is a popular game in Africa. A version for sale in the United States has brought the game to many American families as well. But you don't have to buy anything to have fun with this game. Just find some pebbles and play!

16 Which is the first step in playing Oware?

○ Take the stones from a pit and set them aside.

○ Drop one stone in each pit.

○ Count the stones to see who has the most.

○ Divide the stones evenly among the pits.

17 Which sentence states a fact?

○ "The African pit-and-pebble game of Oware has many names in many languages."

○ "It is easy to learn."

○ "You don't have to buy anything to have fun."

○ "Oware is simple, portable, and fun to play."

18 The kind of player who would most likely do well at this game is the one who —

○ plays most quickly.

○ matches the moves made by the other players.

○ plans ahead.

○ usually has a lot of luck.

19 Which sentence is a generalization?

○ "The game is played on a board."

○ "Many other games can be boring."

○ "The player drops one stone in each pit."

○ "The first player chooses a pit."

20 At the end of the game, what does the Oware board look like?

○ All the pits are empty.

○ There is one stone in each pit.

○ Some pits have a few stones in them.

○ There is an even number of stones in each pit.

Foresman 3

GO ON

Don't Forget—Vote Today!

Don't forget to vote on the school ballot today. There are three questions students may vote on this year.

Question 1 is about choices in the school lunchroom. Many students have said they want more choices, including hamburgers and hot dogs at every lunch. Should we have more meals to choose from each day, or should we let the lunchroom staff plan one meal for each menu?

Question 2 is about the field trip at the end of the school year. We can go to a museum, a play, or a baseball game. The museum is the Winchester Native American Museum. The play is *You're a Good Man, Charlie Brown.* The baseball game is the Astros against the Red Sox. On the ballot, choose the field trip you would like most.

Questions 3 is about the school play. Mr. Engle has suggested three plays. We get to decide which one of them to perform this year. The choices are *Babe: The Big Blue Ox, Story Time,* and *Space Pioneers.* Mark your choice on the ballot.

Be sure to vote today! Very few students voted on the last ballot, and some important decisions were made by a small number of people. It is important that you make your wishes known!

You'll find your ballot on the big table in the lunchroom. Please mark your ballot clearly and put it in the blue box.

We will post the results at the end of the week.

GO ON

21 Which is the best summary of this passage?

○ Many students want hamburgers and hot dogs for lunch every day.

○ Students will vote on choices in the lunch menu, which field trip to take, and which play to perform.

○ The students must choose the field trip they want to take. They can go to a museum, a play, or a baseball game.

○ There are three questions on the school ballot. Ballots are in the blue box.

22 The author of this passage seems to be worried that the students will —

○ make poor choices in the lunchroom.

○ cheat by filling out more than one ballot each.

○ use up all of the ballots.

○ not bother to vote.

23 In what way are the second and third ballot questions alike?

○ In both, students are asked to pick one of three choices.

○ Both involve food.

○ In both, students made up the list of choices.

○ Both affect students every school day.

24 After they have marked their ballots, students should —

○ place them in the blue box.

○ eat lunch.

○ go on a field trip.

○ vote on each question.

25 In this passage, the word <u>post</u> means —

○ to send by mail.

○ a wooden support.

○ to make known by public notice.

○ an army base.

STOP

READING: Phonics

DIRECTIONS
Read the word. Find the word that has the same sound as the underlined letter or letters. Mark the space for your answer.

1 s<u>k</u>in
- ○ show
- ○ send
- ○ speak
- ○ scarf

2 <u>str</u>ength
- ○ treat
- ○ stripe
- ○ squirt
- ○ store

3 sti<u>ll</u>
- ○ hole
- ○ stiff
- ○ sort
- ○ talk

4 <u>j</u>oke
- ○ go
- ○ get
- ○ grape
- ○ giraffe

5 <u>ph</u>one
- ○ life
- ○ pants
- ○ hope
- ○ chin

6 <u>r</u>oom
- ○ when
- ○ wrap
- ○ waist
- ○ wheel

7 <u>c</u>arry
- ○ king
- ○ cereal
- ○ chief
- ○ sun

8 <u>wh</u>en
- ○ how
- ○ write
- ○ hen
- ○ wheat

GO ON

© Scott Foresman 3

9 l**i**p
- ○ line
- ○ will
- ○ stir
- ○ fire

10 cl**ai**m
- ○ mark
- ○ mall
- ○ man
- ○ may

11 s**ui**t
- ○ hurt
- ○ sit
- ○ shut
- ○ new

12 j**oy**
- ○ spoil
- ○ spot
- ○ spout
- ○ spy

13 h**er**
- ○ steer
- ○ cart
- ○ were
- ○ here

GO ON ➡

Foresman 3

DIRECTIONS

Choose the best answer to each question. Mark the space for your answer.

14 Which is a compound word?
- ○ barnyard
- ○ appear
- ○ chimney
- ○ courage

15 What is the base word in the word <u>comfortable</u>?
- ○ table
- ○ for
- ○ able
- ○ comfort

16 What word is formed when you add the suffix -<u>ness</u> to the base word <u>happy</u>?
- ○ happyness
- ○ happness
- ○ hapiness
- ○ happiness

17 What is the prefix in the word <u>unlikely</u>?
- ○ like
- ○ un
- ○ unlike
- ○ ly

GO ON

t Foresman 3

DIRECTIONS

Read each sentence. Choose the correct form of the word to complete each sentence. Mark the space for your answer.

18 *Dark Night* is the _____ movie I have ever seen.
- ○ scarier
- ○ scariest
- ○ scaryer
- ○ scaryest

19 It was about three _____ adventures in a haunted house.
- ○ girls
- ○ girl's
- ○ girls's
- ○ girls'

20 Everyone in the audience _____ at the end.
- ○ clap
- ○ clapped
- ○ claped
- ○ clapping

t Foresman 3

WRITING/GRAMMAR

DIRECTIONS

Read the passage. Choose the word or words that best fit in each numbered blank. Mark the space for your answer.

My grandfather and I went to the circus. We saw three

clowns dressed up as _____. They _____ around in circles and
                (1)   (2)

playing tricks on each other. All of a sudden, one clown _____
                                                (3)

into a big cannon. Then the cannon went off. The clown flew

through the air and landed _____ in a net. It was a great stunt!
                          (4)

1 ○ child
  ○ childs
  ○ children
  ○ childrens

2 ○ running
  ○ was running
  ○ were running
  ○ runned

3 ○ jumping
  ○ jumped
  ○ jump
  ○ will jump

4 ○ most safe
  ○ safer
  ○ safest
  ○ safely

GO ON

DIRECTIONS

Read the passage. Look at the underlined parts. Decide which type of mistake, if any, appears in each underlined part. Mark the space for your answer.

I always have a great time with my dog. <u>Sometimes Lucky and I</u>
                                              (5)
<u>go to jordan park.</u> I throw a stick or a plastic saucer, and he catches

it. <u>Then he brings it back?</u>
      (6)
   <u>One day I threw a saucer, and it sailed too far.</u> It was headed
      (7)
straight for the lake. <u>Watch out, Lucky!</u> I shouted. He jumped into
                           (8)
the air and caught it just in time.

---

5   ○ Spelling
    ○ Capitalization
    ○ Punctuation
    ○ No mistake

6   ○ Spelling
    ○ Capitalization
    ○ Punctuation
    ○ No mistake

7   ○ Spelling
    ○ Capitalization
    ○ Punctuation
    ○ No mistake

8   ○ Spelling
    ○ Capitalization
    ○ Punctuation
    ○ No mistake

tt Foresman 3

DIRECTIONS

Read the passage. Some parts are underlined. The underlined parts may be one of the following:

- **Incomplete sentences**
- **Run-on sentences**
- **Correctly written sentences that should be combined**
- **Correctly written sentences that do not need to be rewritten**

Mark the space beside the best way to write each underlined part. If the underlined part needs no change, mark the choice "No mistake."

Yesterday I tried out a paddle board for the first time.

Amazed at how it rocked with every little wave. I paddled
(9)
slowly away from the beach. A big wave came it knocked me
(10)
over. But I got better at paddling and had a great time.

9
○ Amazed at how it rocked, with every little wave.

○ I was amazed at how it rocked with every little wave.

○ I was amazed at how it rocked, and it rocked with every little wave.

○ No mistake

10
○ A big wave came the wave knocked me over.

○ A big wave came, it knocked me over.

○ A big wave came and knocked me over.

○ No mistake

STOP

tt Foresman 3

WRITING

Think about something special that happened to you during the school year. It might have been something you enjoyed, something you learned, or something that made you feel embarrassed.

Write a personal narrative telling what happened. Tell what you did and how you felt.

Prewriting Notes

t Foresman 3

_____

_____

_____

_____

_____

_____

_____

_____

_____

_____

_____

It Foresman 3

 GO ON

tt Foresman 3

STOP

STUDY SKILLS

DIRECTIONS

Kumiko is writing a report about recycling. She finds a book about recycling. Use the table of contents and part of the index from the book to answer questions 1–2.

Contents

Index

1 In which chapter will Kumiko find information about things that can be made from recycled paper?

○ Chapter 1
○ Chapter 3
○ Chapter 5
○ Chapter 6

2 On what page should Kumiko look for information about recycling plastics?

○ page 3
○ page 18
○ page 23
○ page 29

GO ON

tt Foresman 3

DIRECTIONS
Kumiko takes out a dictionary to look up some words she does not know. Use this part of a dictionary page to answer questions 3–4.

---

recur ▪ reed

re·cur (ri kėr′), *v.* **1** to come up again; occur again; be repeated: *Leap year recurs every four years.* **2** to return in thought or speech: *Seeing old friends made childhood memories recur to them. He recurred to the matter of cost.* ❑ *v.* **re·curred, re·cur·ring.**

re·cur·rence (ri kėr′əns), *n.* occurrence again; repetition; return: *prevent the recurrence of a mistake.*

re·cur·rent (ri kėr′ənt), *adj.* occurring again; repeated; recurring: *recurrent attacks of hay fever.*

re·cy·cle (rē sī′kəl), *v.* to process or treat something so that it can be used again. *Paper, aluminum, and glass products are commonly recycled.* ❑ *v.* **re·cy·cled, re·cycling.**

---

3 Which of these words could be found on this same page of the dictionary?
- ○ rebel
- ○ reason
- ○ refine
- ○ reduce

4 What does <u>recur</u> mean?
- ○ to happen again
- ○ to process or treat something
- ○ to make a speech
- ○ to use something again

GO ON ▶

DIRECTIONS

Choose the best answer to each question about reference sources that Kumiko can use to find information for her report.

5 To find an article about recycling in her area, Kumiko should look in —
- ○ a newspaper.
- ○ an atlas.
- ○ an encyclopedia.
- ○ a textbook.

6 To find information about how plastics were invented, Kumiko should look in —
- ○ an encyclopedia.
- ○ a dictionary.
- ○ an atlas.
- ○ a newspaper.

GO ON

DIRECTIONS
Kumiko found this graph about things made from recycled plastic. Use the graph to help answer questions 7–8.

Use of Recycled PET Plastic in 1997

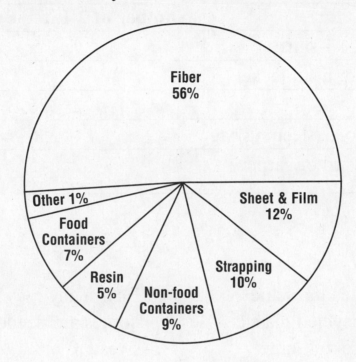

7 In 1997, the greatest amount of PET plastic was used to make —
   ○ fiber.
   ○ strapping.
   ○ food containers.
   ○ sheet and film.

8 What percentage of recycled PET plastic was used to make food containers in 1997?
   ○ 1%
   ○ 7%
   ○ 9%
   ○ 10%

Foresman 3

GO ON

DIRECTIONS

Kumiko found this table about how many recycled PET plastic bottles are needed to make different products. Use the table to help answer questions 9–10.

Item	Number of 2-Liter Bottles Needed
An extra-large T-shirt	5
Soft filling for a ski jacket	5
A sweater	25
Soft filling for 1 sleeping bag	35
One square yard of carpet	45

9 Which requires the same number of recycled plastic bottles as an extra-large T-shirt?

○ soft filling for a sleeping bag

○ a sweater

○ soft filling for a ski jacket

○ one square yard of carpet

10 How many recycled 2-liter bottles are needed to make a sweater?

○ 5 bottles

○ 25 bottles

○ 35 bottles

○ 45 bottles

STOP

Foresman 3

ANSWER KEY

Unit 1 Skills Test

READING: Comprehension

1. bored
2. pretend it was a magic carpet
3. She likes to play make-believe games.
4. tell a funny story about Asha and Reth
5. hangs loosely; wraps
6. see other places
7. won awards for her books
8. She has been writing books since 1986.
9. give information about Cynthia Rylant
10. give
11. hard-working
12. no one dared to bother her
13. foolish
14. entertain with a funny story
15. carried
16. He does not get a lot of mail.
17. wear funny hats
18. has one of the funniest hats
19. invite friends to a party
20. excited

READING: Phonics

21. lot
22. back
23. cup
24. pin
25. rest
26. much
27. bread
28. touch
29. rain
30. these
31. ride
32. cute
33. me
34. lie
35. road
36. ray
37. happen
38. pass
39. water
40. stuff

WRITING/GRAMMAR

1. We didn't catch a single fish.
2. Do fish eat gumdrops?
3. Jane's mom went too.
4. Then they rode on the swan boats.
5. What a day they had!

WRITING

Scoring Guide: Personal Narrative

4 Exemplary
- Flows from beginning to middle to end
- Rich use of details reveals writer's feelings.
- Keen sense of audience and purpose
- Vivid word choice reveals writer's voice.
- Errors do not prevent understanding.

3 Competent
- Clear beginning, middle, end
- Details reveals writer's feelings.
- Sense of audience and purpose
- Word choice reveals writer's voice.
- Errors do not prevent understanding.

2 Developing
- Lacks clear beginning, middle, end
- A few details suggest writer's feelings.
- Lacks clear sense of audience and purpose
- Limited or vague word choice
- Errors may prevent understanding.

1 Emerging
- No movement from beginning to end
- Writer fails to reveal self through details.
- No sense of audience and purpose
- Incorrect or redundant word choice
- Errors prevent understanding.

STUDY SKILLS

1. Chapter 1
2. page 36
3. page 28
4. pages 44–45
5. in the glossary
6. Des Moines
7. 5-D
8. west
9. Jefferson City
10. 4-E

ANSWER KEY

Unit 2 Skills Test

READING: Comprehension

1. ate
2. A farmer scares animals away from his garden.
3. threw
4. He smiles at a rabbit.
5. waking up
6. Americans throw away a lot of garbage and bury it in landfills.
7. how landfills are built
8. soil
9. throw away
10. "We create about four pounds of garbage per person every day."
11. how volcanoes are formed
12. under
13. "Ash from a volcano helps make the soil rich."
14. conduit
15. vent
16. A squirrel talks to a dog.
17. told
18. A fox gets caught in a trap.
19. things to eat and drink
20. afraid

READING: Phonics

21. less
22. could
23. house
24. page
25. boot
26. rice
27. cow
28. such
29. gown
30. wood
31. jump
32. loud
33. tooth
34. boss
35. town
36. shine
37. cake
38. pen
39. bell
40. light

WRITING/GRAMMAR

1. cities
2. Lake Michigan
3. Casper, Wyoming
4. No mistake
5. Darlene's

WRITING

Scoring Guide: Description

4 Exemplary
- Vivid sense words and images
- Ideas clear and focused
- Elaboration with strong details
- Clear, varied, smooth sentences
- Errors do not prevent understanding.

3 Competent
- Includes sense words and images
- Ideas generally clear and focused
- Elaboration with three or more details
- Most sentences varied and smooth
- Errors do not prevent understanding.

2 Developing
- Some sense words; images may not be clear.
- Ideas may lack focus and clarity.
- Elaboration with two or more details
- Simple sentences; sometimes awkward
- Errors may prevent understanding.

1 Emerging
- Few or no sense words or images
- Ideas lack focus and clarity.
- Lacks elaboration
- Incomplete and/or awkward sentences
- Errors prevent understanding.

STUDY SKILLS

1. the unit of money in Japan
2. <u>a</u> in <u>age</u>
3. a place where railroad cars are stored
4. yew
5. to make or become yellow
6. climb
7. join
8. shake
9. mouth
10. thunder

ANSWER KEY

Unit 3 Skills Test

READING: Comprehension

1. cutting down trees
2. correct
3. "The crops turned brown."
4. He took down his fence.
5. A farmer built a fence to keep animals out, but his crops did not grow. The animals gave him food, so he took the fence down.
6. flops into a puddle
7. He was dripping with mud.
8. putting water and soap in a pail
9. a place
10. Hobo plays in a puddle. After getting cleaned up, he sleeps and dreams about puddles.
11. Her feet flew out from under her.
12. useful hints
13. keep her knees bent
14. "She pushed off for a slow, steady glide across the ice."
15. Kasha had trouble skating until Ms. Reid gave her a lesson. Then she learned fast.
16. reading each thermometer
17. to put in a certain spot
18. It gets warmer.
19. a white shirt
20. Use thermometers and paper to find out if a white shirt is cooler than a black one.

READING: Phonics

21. here	31. mushy
22. mark	32. other
23. fair	33. kind
24. jar	34. flower
25. wrap	35. trust
26. knot	36. gold
27. sign	37. mysterious
28. lamb	38. beautiful
29. before	39. surely
30. pitcher	40. silliness

WRITING/GRAMMAR

1. is
2. shared
3. tasted
4. thought
5. will bring

WRITING

Scoring Guide: Comparison/Contrast Paragraph

4 Exemplary
- Clear topic sentence
- Ideas are organized and flow smoothly.
- Transitions show likenesses and differences.
- Clear, varied, smooth sentences
- Errors do not prevent understanding.

3 Competent
- Understandable topic sentence
- Ideas generally organized
- Some transitions
- Most sentences varied and smooth
- Errors do not prevent understanding.

2 Developing
- Attempts to write a topic sentence
- Ideas generally organized
- Could use more transitions
- Simple sentences; sometimes awkward
- Errors may prevent understanding.

1 Emerging
- No topic sentence
- Ideas seem unconnected.
- Few or no transitions
- Incomplete and/or awkward sentences
- Errors prevent understanding.

STUDY SKILLS

1. Vol. 12
2. Vol. 5
3. Vol. 1
4. comedy — comma
5. plum — Plymouth
6. a newspaper
7. an atlas
8. an encyclopedia
9. a dictionary
10. an almanac

ANSWER KEY

Unit 4 Skills Test

READING: Comprehension

1. A plan that seems wise can go wrong.
2. in a meadow
3. sweet
4. fall
5. If you wait too long, you may lose the thing you want.
6. a fable
7. It is better to be safe than sorry.
8. early morning
9. she wanted to take Hank home
10. foolish
11. in their basement
12. Take advice from someone who knows more than you.
13. wonderful
14. He wanted to work in a hospital there.
15. She did not have neighbors who spoke Spanish.
16. It has warmer winters.
17. "I have taken a fancy to many American foods."
18. autobiography
19. buy a present for his aunt
20. darken
21. Both cost less than nine dollars.
22. He tried hard.
23. She was rude.
24. tell Mr. Perkins about the two clerks he met

READING: Phonics

25. toys
26. point
27. enjoy
28. voice
29. tore
30. learn
31. four
32. were
33. skate
34. wind
35. crown
36. jump
37. square
38. scrape
39. three
40. string
41. dog's
42. girls'
43. coat's
44. friends'
45. car's

WRITING/GRAMMAR

1. loudest
2. doesn't
3. the
4. faster
5. Center Street

WRITING

Scoring Guide: How-To Report

4 Exemplary
- Task fully defined
- Ample information provided
- Words like *first* indicate order of steps.
- Clear sentences guide readers.
- Errors do not prevent understanding.

3 Competent
- Task defined
- Adequate information provided
- Words like *first* indicate order of steps.
- Sentences are generally clear.
- Errors do not prevent understanding.

2 Developing
- Limited definition of task
- May have gaps in information
- Needs more words to show order of steps
- Sentences could be clearer.
- Errors may prevent understanding.

1 Emerging
- No attempt to define task
- Inadequate information provided
- No words used to show order of steps
- Sentences lack clarity and confuse reader.
- Errors prevent understanding.

STUDY SKILLS

1. 11
2. walking
3. 8
4. often
5. 16%
6. almost never
7. Your Health
8. four
9. Lesson 2
10. "How Exercise Helps You"

ANSWER KEY

Unit 5 Skills Test

READING: Comprehension

1. The tracks melt away.
2. problem and solution
3. "Winter is an excellent time to study animal tracks."
4. show what animal tracks look like
5. "During the summer, this rabbit's fur is brown."
6. contrast
7. "During his lifetime he photographed 5,381 snowflakes."
8. in the order that things happened
9. "Bentley's book was a great gift to the world."
10. read Bentley's book
11. giving dates and periods of time
12. give information about Wilson Bentley
13. He will tell Chief Joseph what he has learned.
14. to show the way
15. a large rabbit
16. tell a story about a young man
17. historical fiction
18. "The smoke rising from his fire looked like shadowy men."
19. make another phone call
20. realistic fiction
21. rip or pull apart
22. persuade readers to call for information
23. "But now she was a bird getting ready to fly."
24. seven days

READING: Phonics

25. ache	36. dis-
26. home	37. tried
27. while	38. stopping
28. rake	39. easiest
29. came	40. hotter
30. hand	41. nicest
31. whose	42. cards
32. lake	43. stones
33. dis-	44. thieves
34. im-	45. mice
35. non-	

WRITING/GRAMMAR

1. I	4. near
2. We	5. but
3. his	

WRITING

Scoring Guide: Research Report

4 Exemplary
• Strong introduction and conclusion
• Information complete and well organized
• Good use of sources
• Clear, varied, smooth sentences
• Errors do not prevent understanding.

3 Competent
• Good introduction and conclusion
• Information complete and organized
• Good use of sources
• Most sentences varied and smooth
• Errors do not prevent understanding.

2 Developing
• Attempts an introduction and conclusion
• May have gaps in information
• Source is not well used
• Simple sentences; sometimes awkward
• Errors may prevent understanding.

1 Emerging
• No introduction and conclusion
• Inadequate information provided
• Source is not well used
• Incomplete and/or awkward sentences
• Errors prevent understanding.

STUDY SKILLS

1. Palouse
2. Flathead
3. go to the index or table of contents
4. Texas
5. Zuni and Apache
6. Apache
7. Oklahoma
8. 1877
9. Chief Joseph died
10. 2,000

ANSWER KEY

Unit 6 Skills Test

READING: Comprehension

1. "Space projects cost a lot of money."
2. A space station will be built in space.
3. space shuttles are used a lot by NASA
4. save money
5. to come down from the air; come to rest
6. Bluebird jumped into a lake.
7. at a lake
8. long ago
9. Coyote fell in the dirt.
10. to look; pay attention to
11. in a bedroom
12. reading and drawing with Nana
13. Keisha tells Nana some news.
14. many old people can't do all the things they used to do
15. a sudden attack of illness
16. at Tomás's house
17. "Letters always get lost in the mail."
18. He keeps losing things.
19. Tomás finds the letter from Mrs. Gomez and gives it to his mom.
20. a tool used for writing

READING: Phonics

21. draw
22. suit
23. stall
24. flew
25. chew
26. lawn
27. caught
28. bruise
29. thought
30. appear
31. place
32. truth
33. dis
34. un
35. less
36. able
37. un • der • stand
38. hope • less
39. some • thing
40. um • brel • la

WRITING/GRAMMAR

1. No mistake
2. Now Nigel and his cousin want to be astronauts.
3. January 12, 2000
4. No mistake
5. She said, "Tell Nikki to bring a sleeping bag."

WRITING

Scoring Guide: Persuasive Letter

4 Exemplary
- Clear purpose and sense of audience
- Strong persuasive words
- Convincing supporting details
- Correct letter format
- Errors do not prevent understanding.

3 Competent
- Shows purpose and sense of audience
- Persuasive words
- Good supporting details
- Correct letter format
- Errors do not prevent understanding.

2 Developing
- Shows some sense of purpose and audience
- Words are only mildly persuasive.
- Some details
- Follows main parts of letter format
- Errors may prevent understanding.

1 Emerging
- Shows no sense of purpose and audience
- Language is not persuasive.
- Few or no details
- Does not follow letter format
- Errors prevent understanding.

STUDY SKILLS

1. in a school gym
2. 5:00 P.M.
3. 10:00 A.M.
4. cookies
5. persuade people to go to the sale
6. a news story
7. "Yard Sale"
8. an editorial
9. sports
10. "Student Wins Spelling Bee"

Answer Key

End-of-Year Skills Test

READING: Comprehension

1. had been to the waterfall before
2. He will think about why it is bothering him.
3. spoiled; made unclean
4. "Both he and his horse were moving as slowly as snails."
5. in a desert
6. Other lakes may be deeper or longer, but Lake Superior has the greatest area of any freshwater lake.
7. It is entirely in the United States.
8. comparison and contrast
9. Africa
10. filled with salt water
11. The car's air conditioning shuts down.
12. "It's a great book."
13. funny
14. "get on each other's nerves"
15. persuade Maria to read *The Sand and the Sun*
16. Divide the stones evenly among the pits.
17. "The African pit-and-pebble game of Oware has many names in many languages."
18. plans ahead
19. "Many other games can be boring."
20. All the pits are empty.
21. Students will vote on choices in the lunch menu, which field trip to take, and which play to perform.
22. not bother to vote
23. In both, students are asked to pick one of three choices.
24. place them in the blue box
25. to make known by public notice

READING: Phonics

1. scarf
2. stripe
3. hole
4. giraffe
5. life
6. wrap
7. king
8. wheat
9. will
10. may
11. new
12. spoil
13. were
14. barnyard
15. comfort
16. happiness
17. un
18. scariest
19. girls'
20. clapped

WRITING/GRAMMAR

1. children
2. were running
3. jumped
4. safely
5. Capitalization
6. Punctuation
7. No mistake
8. Punctuation
9. I was amazed at how it rocked with every little wave.
10. A big wave came and knocked me over.

WRITING

Scoring Guide: Personal Narrative

4 Exemplary
- Flows from beginning to middle to end
- Rich use of details reveals writer's feelings.
- Keen sense of audience and purpose
- Vivid word choice reveals writer's voice.
- Errors do not prevent understanding.

3 Competent
- Clear beginning, middle, end
- Details reveal writer's feelings.
- Sense of audience and purpose
- Word choice reveals writer's voice.
- Errors do not prevent understanding.

2 Developing
- Lacks clear beginning, middle, end
- A few details suggest writer's feelings.
- Lacks clear sense of audience and purpose
- Limited or vague word choice
- Errors may prevent understanding.

1 Emerging
- No movement from beginning to end
- Writer fails to reveal self through details.
- No sense of audience and purpose
- Incorrect or redundant word choice
- Errors prevent understanding.

STUDY SKILLS

1. Chapter 5
2. page 18
3. reduce
4. to happen again
5. a newspaper
6. an encyclopedia
7. fiber
8. 7%
9. soft filling for a ski jacket
10. 25 bottles